DUNYA MIKHAIL work
before she was forced to f
War Works Hard was shortlisted
of a Wave Outside the Sea won the 2010 Arab A
Award for poetry. Dunya Mikhail has received a   ggenhei
Fellowship, a Knight Foundation grant, a Kresge Fellowship
and the United Nations Human Rights Award for Freedom of
Writing. She works as a special lecturer of Arabic at Oakland
University in Michigan.

PRAISE FOR *THE BEEKEEPER OF SINJAR*

"Haunting and captivating – a powerful portrait of courage"
Elle UK

"War memoirs tend to be written by soldiers; civilian
voices are seldom heard. *The Beekeeper of Sinjar* by the
Iraqi-American poet and journalist Dunya Mikhail, is a
rare and powerful exception … This is one story among
many, which together illuminate a human catastrophe that
might otherwise be a mere footnote to the still-unfolding
consequences of the Iraq war. Mikhail's gifts as a poet infuse
these narratives with unexpected beauty." *New York Times
Review of Books*

"The stories in *The Beekeeper of Sinjar* are reminiscent of
tales of escapees on the US's Underground Railroad of the
mid-1800s or during the Holocaust. The book is a paean for
coexistence in a multi-ethnic, multi-religious, multilingual
Iraq. Powerful and difficult." *The National*

"Iraqi journalist and poet Mikhail lays bare the agonizing experiences of the Yazidi people at the hands of ISIS in this visceral account of the outskirts of modern-day Iraq ... Powerful and heartbreaking, this work lets the survivors tell their stories and highlights the courage of those risking their lives to rescue others." *Publishers Weekly*

"A brutally important, electrifying, and lyrical true story" *Foreword*

"Remarkable. A child's perspective mingles freely with the poet's mature voice, both baffled by the paradoxes of so much beauty and so much destruction." *Washington Post*

"Shakespeare would have enjoyed the poetry of Dunya Mikhail, who has spoken of love as a response to a war-torn world – an aesthetic, a value, and a practice." Elizabeth Toohey, *Christian Science Monitor*

ALSO BY DUNYA MIKHAIL

Diary of a Wave Outside the Sea
The Iraqi Nights
The War Works Hard

Dunya Mikhail

THE BEEKEEPER
OF SINJAR

Translated from the Arabic
by Dunya Mikhail and Max Weiss

This paperback edition published in 2019

First published in Great Britain in 2018 by Serpent's Tail,
an imprint of Profile Books Ltd
3 Holford Yard
Bevin Way
London WC1X 9HD
www.serpentstail.com

First published in the USA in 2018 by New Directions Books, New York

Originally published in Arabic as *Fi Suq al-Sabaya* by Al Mutawassit

10 9 8 7 6 5 4 3 2 1

Typeset in Sabon by MacGuru Ltd
Printed and bound by CPI Group (UK) Ltd, Croydon CR0 4YY

A CIP record for this book can be obtained from the British Library.

ISBN 978 1 78816 129 9
eISBN 978 1 78283 480 9

A Simple Word of Thanks

Thank you to those women who escaped the clutches of Daesh for their willingness to speak about the details of their suffering, despite the fact that deep wounds don't speak, they can only be felt.

Thank you to those victims who were killed but didn't die, who came back to tell us their stories.

Thank you to all those people in the camps for their hearts, which are as open to the air as their tents.

Thank you to Abdullah Shrem, a hero of our time.

CONTENTS

The Beekeeper of Sinjar

N

In America they say teachers have eyes in the backs of their heads. As I write on the blackboard I can see my students behind me writing Arabic letters from right to left, as they're supposed to. Usually I introduce each new letter with a story, some pronunciation drills, and writing exercises, while using words that contain the letter as examples. But today it's time for N (noon), and that letter is no longer neutral like all the others, nor is its story like any other. And so I find myself pausing today, uncharacteristically, standing there for a moment before introducing the letter, spending more time with N than with any other letter in my entire life.

I didn't ask my students if they knew that the letter was now being written in red on doors, notifying residents that they must leave their homes or else face death. Reduced to an N, those *Nasara* – "Christians" – were shaken out of sleep by megaphones blaring all over town that they had twenty-four hours to get out, and that they couldn't take anything with them; and just like that, with the stroke of a red marker across their doors, they would have to abandon the houses they'd lived in for over 1,500 years. They'd leave their doors ajar and turn their backs on houses that would become *Property of the Islamic State*. But I didn't explain any of this. My job is to teach Arabic, nothing more. The sentiments that letter was

1

inspiring in me as I traced it out brought on a slightly exaggerated pause. "We write the letter like this ... a semicircle ... with a dot on top." I write it again and again, all along the length of the blackboard: a chasm and a dot, a chasm and a dot. The students also write out the letter; in their notebooks it looks like a crescent moon with a tiny star. "A beautiful letter, with a certain ring to it," I say, offering examples: person, *nas*; resonance, *raniin*; homeland, *wattan*.

If I were to tell them what was on my mind, I'd speak of Nadia, the young Yazidi woman who'd told me how she'd escaped from Daesh. Maybe they don't know anything about the Yazidis, who had been forced to flee their homes, who had taken shelter in a cave on the outskirts of Sinjar, the mountain that was less cruel to them than man.

I felt my students were too delicate to hear how young ladies were sold in warehouses after being inspected like watermelons – buyers would select the ones they wanted after smelling the girls carefully.

According to Daesh's price list, Nadia was worth 100,000 dinars (about eighty-five American dollars), based on her age, twenty-eight years old. But she could also be "gifted" free of charge to one of their emirs, "in recognition of his jihad," a gift made in hopes that he wouldn't keep her very long. I came to know Nadia through a Yazidi journalist friend of mine. She spoke with me on the phone in Kurdish, a language I don't speak, although I understood her pain fluently. Listening to her, I imagined a butterfly's wings fluttering inside of her voice.

*   *   *

Her cousin Abdullah translated what Nadia said into Arabic for me:

I was at home when my husband, moving the telephone away from his ear, told us, "We have to leave now, Daesh is nearby." That was a Sunday morning, the first Sunday in August, when we fled our home in the village of Sawlakh, east of Sinjar, along with our neighbors and their families. I walked with my husband and our three children alongside a caravan of nearly two hundred people, which included breastfeeding children such as my own youngest son. It was very hot outside and we had departed without any water or food or diapers. We headed up into the mountains, stopping every hour so that we could rest a bit, especially for the sake of the exhausted children. We found a vegetable farm and stopped to pick tomatoes – we were so thirsty. That's when we were surrounded by Daesh fighters.

First they loaded the men, then the women and children, onto big trucks, taking us to Mosul. The whole way there we were crying and screaming, even as they wrote down our names and ages. When they unloaded us in Mosul, they separated the virgins from the married women; they also set apart children over the age of twelve. Then they took us to a school in Talafar where we stayed for eighteen days, studying Quran. They forced us to recite verses in that filthy place, even as we were dying of hunger and thirst. They told us that we were infidels, that we must convert to Islam because it's "the true faith," and that we'd have to get married. Then they transferred us to another building near Raqqa, in Syria, where they put us up for auction. The men would sometimes bid one dollar more than the price we were announced for – we'd hear the auctioneer call out, "200 dollars, do I hear 201? Nobody? Anyone? Sold." They handed me a slip of paper with the name of the buyer written on it, informing me that it was my marriage certificate. I had no idea what they'd done with my husband and his father and his brother and all the rest of our relatives who'd been with us in the convoy. The man who'd bought me told me I was now his wife. "Isn't it forbidden to marry married women?" I asked him. "Not Yazidis," he replied.

He took me and my three children to a four-story building in the Tishreen Dam region. He was a Chechen man who spoke modern standard Arabic. I didn't even know how to read Arabic but he forced me to recite the Quran after him. He would beat my children right in front of me: "They don't know how to read as well as they ought to." The worst thing was that he threatened to take my children away from me if I didn't do what he told me. When he ordered me to bathe, I understood what this meant, and I obeyed him to protect my children, who were six, five, and one. He raped me right there in front of them. Sometimes his friends would pass us around for a day or two, like presents being borrowed, a practice they called "rent." They spoke amongst themselves in languages I couldn't understand, and talked to us in Arabic, but it wasn't anything like the Arabic spoken by Arabs in our country. Daesh Arabic was much clearer, as if they were reading out of a book. We stayed there for three months, and during that time we made hundreds of rockets. My children and I worked twelve hours a day for them. They gave my five-year-old daughter the most dangerous job, tying together the detonation lines. At any moment a mistake could explode the bomb right in

her face. Along with another female captive, I would load
the rockets into a truck. She was a Yazidi from my village,
and she had two children. We became so close that we con-
spired to escape together. Friendship was our only hope. At
first the man who bought me would lock the door every day
when he left, but after three months he began leaving the
door unlocked, which made it seem that he had come to
believe I was his devoted Muslim wife. One day he told me
he was going off to fight, and that he'd be back in three days.
My heart started pounding at the sight of the door, the door
that would be open to me for three full days. I ran to my
friend who was in another room with her two children, and
whispered that we were getting out of there. "Don't leave
me here, please," she said. "Like we promised," I reminded
her, "either we die or we get out of here together."

Her Daeshi owner wasn't there, but he could be back
at any moment because he never told her he was going
off to fight. I said I'd try to get ahold of my cousin in
Dohuk to help us. Right away I went out into the street and
walked to an Internet café I'd heard about. I mustered up
the courage to ask the shopkeeper for help, telling him I
needed to make a phone call even though I didn't have any
money. Thankfully he let me use the phone. I called my
cousin Abdullah, and he immediately asked me, "Where
are you?" I didn't know exactly so I asked the shopkeeper:
"Mosque Street," he said, "it's a little neighborhood with
only one mosque, across from the bakery – everyone knows
the bakery."

Abdullah's voice was like a life raft: "I'll send a driver
tomorrow at 10 a.m. Wait at the bakery, and if he tells you
Abdullah sent him, get in the car."

"But my friend and her two children are with me," I told him, "and she might not be able to get away tomorrow. I'll have to ask her and get back to you." I thanked the shopkeeper and asked him if it would be possible to make another call a little while later. He nodded. I quickly returned to the house, and went back and forth between my children and my girlfriend until evening, when she found that her man wasn't going off to fight the next day but the day after. As soon as I heard this, I returned to the café and the kind man handed me the phone before I could even ask to use it. "The day after tomorrow – will that work?" I asked Abdullah, gasping. "Of course," he answered, "the day after tomorrow. Same time, same place."

The seven of us stood in front of the bakery with both anxiety and hope. Twenty minutes passed and none of us moved. There was someone at the entrance to the bakery who was glancing at us from time to time. I walked toward him and asked, "Are you with Abdullah?"

"Yes," he replied, and gestured for us to get into his car. He took us to Manbij province, northeast of Aleppo, then to the Euphrates. The plan was for us to cross over to Kobani in a skiff. But we saw dead people lying in the road, which sent our children into a panic, making them shake and cry. I felt like I was going to throw up and my friend covered her eyes.

The driver had to take us back to Manbij, where we spent the night in a house whose inhabitants seemed to have fled. The smuggler explained to us that most of the homes there had been abandoned after Daesh's assault. It was a very small house that still smelled of people, as if they had just left. We stayed the night there, but too nervous that the Daeshis would find us, we counted the minutes until morning, unable to sleep. After the smuggler picked us up, we headed for a rural area east of the Euphrates. There he instructed us to get out of the car and walk toward the river. We followed his instructions, continuing our journey on foot. After about half an hour of walking, we heard the sound of gunshots. We hid among the reeds in the marshes, huddled there for hours, afraid of what might happen at any moment. The smuggler was still with us but he had become extremely tense, especially when the children started crying. He ordered us to stay absolutely silent.

Once the sound of gunfire had subsided, we continued walking to the edge of the river, crossing in a skiff over to Kobani, on the Turkish border. There we were greeted by a group of people, mostly women. They took us to a hotel where we were able to rest for a few days. They gave us fresh clothes and then drove us to Dohuk Province in Iraq, where Abdullah and my mother-in-law lived. Now I live with her. She prays every day for the return of her son, my husband, my real husband. I woke up from a nightmare that still wakes me up every night: the man who bought me comes to kidnap me while I'm picking tomatoes. I see myself naked and barefoot, like a newborn or the newly dead.

I never told my students Nadia's story. I simply wrote her name on the chalkboard as an example of a name that starts with the letter N. But the poem that I wrote far from their prying eyes remained wide awake in my room long after I had gone to sleep, like a light I had forgotten to switch off. It begins:

The N on the doors,
the exodus
from houses:
no keys,
no compass,
no words.

THE BEE KINGDOM

A week had passed since my conversation with Nadia. I was trying to resist my desire to call and ask about her. Her voice followed me everywhere I went. On the Internet I searched for "how to learn a foreign language in ten days," but Kurdish wasn't on the list. I scolded myself: if such a thing were possible, I could have sent my students home ten days later.

Finally I called my friend Dakhil, a journalist who was in touch with several Yazidi families in the camps. I asked him if it would be possible to call Nadia again to make sure she was all right, but before I could, he told me that he'd just gotten off the phone with a mother and her children who had escaped from Daesh.

"Is that right?" I asked. "What did they say?"

"Listen. I'll read you a translation of the transcript."

What's your name?
  Hoshyar.
  How old are you, Hoshyar?
  Three.
  Where were you before you came to Baadhra?
  With Daesh.
  Where with Daesh?
  In Syria.

Hoshyar, were you in a madrassa *with Daesh?*
No, I was in one of their houses.
What were you doing in the house?
They were teaching me Quran.
Who was teaching you Quran?
Abu Jihad.
Why were you there?
They made me go with them.
Where did they take you from?
Raqqa.
The man who was teaching you Quran, where was he from?
Russia.
And how did you know he was from Russia?
He told me.
Who else was there with you?
My mom and my sister and three children with their mother.
Did they teach all of you Quran?
Yes. And we built rockets.
What were you building?
Rocket, rocket.
And what do you remember from the Quran?
I was in Syria with Daesh.
I want to know what you can remember from the Quran.
In the Name of God, most gracious, most compassionate, praise be to God, Lord of the two worlds, the gracious, the compassionate, master of the Day of Judgment …
Do you know what that means?
No, no I don't.
Hoshyar, what did they feed you?

Bones. Abu Jihad would eat meat and then give me the bones. I couldn't eat the bones but he used to make me stand on one leg for an hour.

Were you afraid of them?

He told me he could cut my head off if he wanted to.

Why did he say that?

He told me to pray, he said that when I grew up, God willing, I would go fight with Dacsh.

Hoshyar, where are you right now?

In Baadhra.

Is your situation okay right now? Better than being with Daesh?

I'm at home. I'm good.

Thank you, Hoshyar. Could you hand the phone to your sister?

Hello.

How are you, Rula?

Fine.

How old are you?

Seven.

Can you tell me what you did when you were with Daesh?

They beat me while we made rockets for them.

What kind? And how did you make them?

TNT. From chemicals.

Did you also study Quran and prayer?

Yes.

Did you understand the words you were memorizing?

No.

Who was your teacher?

Daesh.

What was the name of the person who taught you?

Abu Jihad.

Did you learn how to pray?

Yes, but now I want to forget.

All right, Rula, can you give the phone to your mother?

Hello.

Hello, Miss Raghda. Are you from Kocho?

Yes.

When did they take you?

I don't know when. It was when we fled from Sinjar. For two weeks we were surrounded by Daesh. They killed a lot of our people.

After they kidnapped you from Kocho and killed a lot of your people, where did they take you?

First they took the men and killed them. They held us in some building until one in the morning. Then they brought a bus and took all of the girls away, and separated the elderly.

About how many of you were there?

Sixty or seventy.

Everyone was an adult?

Mostly. Some weren't even healthy adults, but disabled.

They were from Kocho …?

No, they killed all the men from Kocho. They took us to Sinjar, where they'd also taken the rest. Then to Talafar. They kept us there for three months. We were thirsty and hungry the whole time. They would only give us one chunk of bread per day. Then they took us to Syria.

And what happened in Syria?

They sold us.

Who did they sell you to?

They sold us from one person to another, until Abu Jihad held onto us so that we could make rockets.

Yes, the children told me. How did you make them?
We boiled them on the stove.
What were you boiling?
Chemicals.
What were they exactly?
Refined sugar powder and chemicals they told us they got near the Turkish border.
How much time did it take to make the rockets?
I made ten or twelve rockets a day for five months.
What kind of rockets? Did it have a shell or was it more like a grenade?
It had a shell. They forced Rula and Hoshyar to make four rockets per day. If there was any defect in the rocket he'd beat them with electrical cables. That was the hardest thing for me. I wanted to kill myself. I pleaded with him not to beat them but he told me he didn't care about anything but the rockets.
What language did he speak?
He spoke Russian with his friends and Arabic with me.
When did you get away, and how?
A month and a half ago. There was a woman who had three children in Daesh's house with us. We came from the same region, and she became my best friend there. She and her children were also making rockets. We'd place them side by side in the car, filling it up with fifty or sixty rockets. One day Abu Jihad told us that he was going off to fight but that he'd be back. My friend called her relative, and she would have been able to get away the very next day but she waited an extra day for me, until Abu Jihad had left. Every minute in captivity cost a lot and yet she waited a whole day so that I could go with her. I'll never forget her generosity, never. My

friend was able to use the telephone at a coffee shop in the neighborhood. Luckily the owners weren't with Daesh. We fled to Kobani in a skiff, where some people greeted us and told us that they were from the People's Defense Brigades.

All right, thank you very much. I'm happy you are all free.

My family – my mother and my father and my brother and my husband's family – are all missing.

We all hope they're safe, too.

After listening to the recording I called Abdullah and asked him, "What's the name of Nadia's friend who escaped with her? Is it Raghda?"

"Yes. How'd you know?"

"Are both of them in Dohuk right now?"

"Yeah. They talk on the telephone every day. As you know, they have some painful shared memories."

"How are the children?"

"They're still shaken up by what happened. For example … well, I better not say."

"Please. I'm a grown woman. You can tell me."

"All right. Yesterday I went to see Nadia and her kids. She's my cousin. I found it strange that her daughter would say to her, *Mama, around this time you were taking off your clothes.* And her younger son kept repeating, *Allahu Akbar*, just like that, every minute or so. Poor Nadia told them: *We have to forget. We're all very tired and we simply have to forget.*"

"Is there anything we can do to help? I feel horrible not doing anything."

"The best thing you can do is write about our suffering."

"Thank you so much for rescuing those kidnapped girls."

"I used to do business in Iraq and Syria, but ever since the Daesh disaster started, my work has become saving female captives. My phone rings off the hook. Sometimes Daesh men themselves will sell the women to me. Yesterday I rescued an entire family. I didn't get to sleep until they finally arrived safely at four in the morning. Can you hear that ringing? Someone's calling right now."

"Yes, please, go – we can talk some other time."

"Thanks. Call whenever you like."

The next day I was putting an orange in my shopping bag when Abdullah called me. I left the orange and the other items in a shopping cart and left the store.

"Hello? I'm sorry I had to cut our conversation short yesterday."

"I totally understand – and deeply admire the work you're doing."

"It was another escaped woman on the run calling. We found her this morning at dawn, thank God."

"That's fantastic. I'm so glad to hear she got away. Was she alone?"

"Yes. The problem is …"

"What?"

"The man who raped her also got her pregnant. We're conservative families, as you know, and it's a big problem for a girl to leave a virgin and come back pregnant. Nobody wants to have the children of terrorists."

"It wasn't her choice."

"I know. Our spiritual leader Baba Sheikh issued a statement declaring that our girls running away from Daesh were helpless, powerless, yet brave in resisting terrorism, which is why their honor cannot be impugned even if their hymens have been damaged."

Is that pregnant survivor going to get rid of her child? I wondered to myself. *If she has him, will he ever seem as beautiful in her eyes as other children are in the eyes of their mothers? Or would she always see him as a painful memory growing alongside her? Had his father ever been an innocent child or had he always been broken, oozing with poison? How had he learned to pray while he cut off people's heads and raped young girls?*

"Are there rehabilitation services available to surviving girls?"

"Our area is poor, as you know, but there are physical therapy sessions for the girls because they suffer from pain all the time. Sometimes they're overcome with fits that are like epilepsy."

Their souls haven't yet moved on, they never will, I thought to myself as I listened to Abdullah. *That's why their bodies hurt so much. Staying alive doesn't mean permanent survival. Anyway, what is survival when the calamity survives along with you? To survive all alone is the worst kind of survival.*

"In Iraq I heard that the Yazidis had strange customs," I told Abdullah, changing the subject, "and to tell you the truth, all of us Iraqis have strange customs, as you know."

"Some people believe that we worship fire, but actually we worship light, which is why we face the sun when we pray. If you visit the Palmyra ruins inside the Aleppo Citadel, you'll find this inscription on one of the stones: *Whoever built the Aleppo Citadel must have worshipped the sun.*"

"The sun deity was one of our Babylonian ancestors. There was democracy back then – people could choose which male or female god they wanted to worship. One of their customs took place on New Year's Day, when they would smack the king's cheek in front of his people so hard that he would start crying. They believed his tears were a good omen for the new year. As for my own customs ... I write poetry. All my other habits are good ones."

"I thought poetry was a good habit. It's not?" he asked.

"Well, perhaps not when you're obsessed with it night and day."

"I used to be obsessed with beekeeping, but ever since we've had our Daesh problem I've been distracted from the bees. Freeing people from those savages has become my daily concern."

"So from bees to beasts."

"I used to have a huge garden in Sinjar where I would tend to the beehives for hours on end, especially on Fridays – discovering the secrets of the bees, their meticulous organization, their harmony with nature. The movements of the queen bee up above, her superior flying abilities compared to the males amazed me, made me profoundly appreciate all the women in my life – especially the queen mother – because her loss would completely disorient the colony. In the end, the females surround the males and expel them from the hive because they're not good for anything other than pollination. That's some justice, isn't it? In our society women work and sacrifice for others without getting what they deserve, without enjoying the same privileges as men. Women are oppressed even outside the world of Daesh, which has nothing whatsoever to do with rational human life, of course. I had experience as a businessman, which required a reputation, many business relationships, and knowledge of the roads. With the money I made selling honey in Iraq and Syria I was able to help save female captives – and I rely upon the same skills in my new work. I cultivated a hive of transporters and smugglers from both sexes to save our queens, the ones Daeshis call *sabaya*, sex slaves. We worked like in a beehive, with extreme care and well-planned initiatives."

"Actually it seems to me that males do more than just pollinate. You save queens, for example ... I mean, female captives," I said.

"That's true, but our hive includes women, too, and they have a big part to play in the rescue operation. At the moment I need to be careful not to talk about the specifics of our work, for their own protection."

"So you gave up beekeeping because you're too busy smuggling families away from Daesh?"

"Beekeeping's just a hobby. What I'm doing now can't be described. I can't explain the feeling I get when I welcome back runaway girls, when they are reunited with their families. We all cry together, overcome with a mixture of joy and outrage. For the sake of that moment, that moment of reunion, I spend most of the day answering calls for help from voices that tell me where their prisons are located. So much of the time the families of the kidnapped can't be found, and those who can don't have much because they fled with nothing but the clothes they were wearing, leaving behind their homes and their farms and their animals. The smugglers who help us are working for a wage, and that's their right."

"And who pays them?" I asked.

"The people in our region help one another. They're in each others' debt. But sometimes I pay the drivers out of my own pocket, and then I get reimbursed by the Office of Kidnapped Affairs, no matter how much the rescue mission costs. In the Office of Kidnapped Affairs, they listen to the survivors and write down reports, but they don't fund the operation until the girls are brought back, and sometimes they even pay by installments later. But money's not going to stop us from doing whatever we can, even if we have to make special arrangements. Our work isn't without danger, of course. Daesh gruesomely executed one of our drivers when he was caught. We were extremely sad to lose him. He was a young man, and I depended on him very much. In fact, up until now, we've lost twelve smugglers."

"How?"

"Sometimes Daesh will propose letting the sabaya return to their families in exchange for a large sum of money. Those who are serious will release their sabaya in exchange for the money; yet there are others who claim they're willing to go through with the exchange but then ambush the go-between when he shows up, killing him despite their previously agreed-upon arrangement. About twenty-five percent of direct purchases from Daesh ended up with our smugglers getting ambushed. There are also Daeshi infiltrators among the transporters, but this isn't clear until it's too late.

"Those smugglers must get a large cut. Why else would they dangerously risk their lives?"

"Some of the smugglers I work with used to run cigarettes. In the regions under Daesh's control, smuggling cigarettes was no less dangerous than smuggling female captives."

"Is smoking forbidden by Daesh?"

"It's a major crime. They'll even chop off the hand of anyone who uses tobacco, in whatever form."

"I didn't know that."

"Those cigarette runners would get paid a certain fee for

the danger of their job, which is why they got an even larger cut when they shifted to smuggling captives. Not just because the cost is higher in relation to the danger involved but also because the emotional yield is so great – there's a human value even greater than the material cost."

"How would the rescue operations actually take place?"

"It would start with a phone call, a kidnapped woman trying to reach her family. Then the family would call me. I advised most people around here with my number not to waste any time exchanging extended pleasantries – you know how long our greetings can be. But of course, I fully sympathize with how it must feel for a person to make a call like that. I instruct the family to give the captive my telephone number so that I can make arrangements with her directly. Then we come up with a plan based on where she is. I use Google Maps to scope out the area – the old map of Syria I used back when I was selling honey is no good anymore because many of those regions have changed. Now I know all the neighborhoods in Raqqa, building by building. When the captive calls me, I pick a specific rendezvous point and a code word, informing her that it's safe to get in the car with the driver who'll pick her up. Once they get far enough away, she'll be moved into a safe house, the same houses where smugglers warehoused cigarettes in the past. She'll stay there for a few days, until the commotion caused by her disappearance dies down a bit. During that time the man who calls himself her master might try to track her down and punish her. Daesh's police won't go near women, though, because they are part of Muslim households. After two or three days the driver will come back to the safe house and they'll continue their journey by car, then on foot for another five or six hours. Sometimes the operation will include crossing the river to Turkey in a skiff and, finally, spending about twelve hours in another car in order to reach the northern border of Iraq, where her family will finally greet her. Sometimes I'll follow the mission step by step; sometimes I cross over into Syria to meet with the smugglers, guiding and encouraging them. There's no need for me to welcome back those captives but often I tag along with the family to the border region between Iraq and Syria because I love being a part of these moments. It's indescribable, everyone bursting with ecstasy and tears and hugs; I've witnessed this over seventy times, and every time I can't keep myself from crying.

"Can you remember the first time you saved one of the girls?"

"In October 2014, I got a call from my brother's daughter Marwa, who told me she'd been kidnapped in the Raqqa area. *Bazda*, I told her, which means get out of there, in Kurdish. Six days later she called me again to tell me she'd run away and that she was safe in the home of a Syrian family. She had stolen a key from a Daeshi woman; this woman used to guard Marwa, occasionally biting her, provoking her by picking fights, preventing her from doing anything, even dying. Marwa has scars from the time she tried to kill herself by slitting her wrists – but this woman saved her first and beat her afterward. Marwa opened the door at four in the morning, then closed it behind her and walked out into the street, flagged down a cab and got in. The taxi driver was stunned. As you know it's rare to find a young lady hailing a taxi in the street at such an early hour. *Where are you going?* he asked her. She broke down in tears, telling him that she had just escaped from Daesh. *Kill me please, I beg you, just don't take me back to them.*

"*I can take you to a neighborhood where the clans are sure*

to offer you shelter, he said. *When they open the door, tell
them: 'I'm at your mercy.' Arab clans won't turn away anyone
who knocks on their door and says that*. Dawn was extremely
quiet as Marwa approached a large house and knocked on the
front door.

"A woman opened the door. As soon as she listened to
Marwa's story she invited her inside. But when the woman's
husband heard that she had run away from Daesh he refused
to take her in. He didn't want to shoulder the responsibility;
he said that he would have to hand her over to the police. The
wife pleaded with her husband to just let the girl be on her
way; eventually she apologized as she said goodbye to Marwa
at the door. Marwa headed somewhere else, this time knock-
ing on the door of a smaller house. A man opened the door
with his wife and children behind him. When she told them she
was running away from Daesh they invited her inside. They sat
down in a circle around her and asked her to tell them what
had happened. She wept even as they tried to calm her down,
telling her they weren't going to abandon her. Their house and
their furniture signaled extreme poverty – they didn't even have
a telephone. They promised that as soon as the shops opened
in the morning they'd take her to the Internet café so she could
use the phone. When Marwa called me, I didn't have a func-
tioning network yet, but I decided to make a few calls and
find her a smuggler. Marwa ended up staying with that family
for fifteen days. They shared their food with her and told her
repeatedly that she was safe with them. By the time I found a
smuggler we'd run into a snag: the owner of the Internet café
found out that she'd escaped from Daesh and threatened the
generous family that he would send her back if they didn't
pay him $7,500. The family agreed to the ransom even though

they had nothing, asking the man to give them time to scrape the money together. The members of the family went from house to house, managing to raise $7,000. When they went to give the money to the Internet café owner, they asked him to forgive the remaining five hundred; he agreed and let Marwa leave with the driver. Marwa came back alone, without her mother or father or sisters or brothers. My brother and my sister and fifty-six members of my family, including cousins, are still missing."

"Where were you when all of this happened, Abdullah? I mean, when Daesh attacked the area?" I asked.

"We were all in Sinjar. We lived in the same area. We saw each other almost every day. But at three in the morning on August 3, 2014, we heard the booming sound of artillery. We had never heard such blasts, even in times of war. Twenty-eight of us gathered together – my mother, my siblings, and their families – all of us hesitant to flee. It isn't so easy for a person to give up their home. After four hours of waiting, we set off in a convoy. There were hundreds of us, including Muslims who'd lived in the same region alongside us for hundreds of years. It was like Judgment Day, people walking to God knows where, some of them barefoot, clutching their children or carrying elderly people on their backs. We couldn't take too much with us but I grabbed four bottles of honey. We spent seven days like that: every morning our breakfast consisted of that honey, but the children didn't like to eat it. They would cry because the whole situation wasn't comfortable for them. Then we had to walk for seven hours to reach the mountaintop. Our water had run out. People can die from thirst in that time of the year. The strange thing was that a pleasant breeze came to us from

time to time, a soft wind that saved us from dryness in that difficult time. Still, a lot of people died on the journey, including
the ill, whose families had to leave them behind. Even though
my mother had been recovering from a heart surgery a few
days earlier, she walked those many hours. For her sake we'd
stop every so often to let her rest, without ever making her
feel like she was slowing us down. A blind man and his family,
including his only child, joined our group. The blind man told
us that his son was a miracle who'd blessed the family after
they spent forty years trying to conceive. We shared a meal
with them, scraping together whatever food they had with the
honey we had left.

"After another two days of walking we came upon a farm
with cucumbers and tomatoes, which seemed like a luxury, so
we rested there for a little while. We heard rumors that Sinjar
was now secure, that Daesh had been defeated, so some families in our convoy decided to turn around and go home, but I
was among those who decided not to return. After hours of
walking we reached the Karsi region, an area known for its
tobacco farming, which was the source of its people's income:
it was the reaping season but this year the fields had been left to
rot. The familiar sight of goats and small farms in the mountains was calming, but it was the calm before the storm because
we later heard that those who had tried to go home were captured by Daesh after the withdrawal of Peshmerga forces. My
mother started pounding on her heart, which had not yet fully
healed from the operation, because my sister, my brother, my
cousins, and all of their families were among those who had
gone back and fallen into the trap. The worst thing I heard was
that Daesh had separated the elderly from everyone else and
had buried them all alive in a large pit; the little children who

refused to be separated from their families were also buried along with them. The Daeshis told the girls that they were taking the elderly folk to a cooler place because it was so hot. I don't understand how we were able to keep moving in such a state of sorrow – our steps weighed down and our cheeks wet with tears. We managed to reach the Syrian border on a road that was being protected by the People's Defense Brigades. To tell you the truth, it was an unusual protection force, as it was mostly made up of women. Throughout that harsh and difficult journey we'd hoped an American or European plane would come to airlift us all to safety, but that never happened. Our convoy had about three hundred and fifty people, including women on the verge of giving birth, disabled people who were barely able to walk, and children who were crying from fear of the unknown. We had lost our sense of humanity but the members of these brigades restored this feeling to us. Their assistance wasn't limited to water, food, and medical attention. They also carried the disabled and the exhausted on their backs. They delivered us to camps in the Zakho region, where they asked us to choose between going to Turkey or remaining in Iraq. Most of us decided to stay in Iraq. We reached Dohuk Province because someone named Shammo al-Howayri had volunteered to host us (more than one hundred people) in a large building next to his house. The building was empty but because of the crisis he furnished it with cots and fans. He brought cow's milk for the children and food from his farm. *I'm sorry I can't do more*, he said, as he fed everyone. There was no toilet in that building so he invited everyone to use the washroom in his own home. Just imagine, all those people using his bathroom and washing their clothes in his machine.

"Eight months later I was able to rent my own place, but

life had lost its flavor. There was a bitterness in my mouth that not even the taste of honey could get rid of. I'm still waiting to hear from my sister so I can rescue her as well. Nevertheless, every day that I save a captive woman I save her, too; every day I greet a survivor I welcome her home, too."

"My brother-in-law's daughter was kidnapped seven years ago, before the age of Daesh," I said. "She was coming home from the market in Baghdad with her mother when she was assaulted by masked men who forced her into their car, leaving her mother's hand still reaching for her. The family had been making preparations to leave Iraq because of the endless violence, but after the kidnapping they decided to stay in the country until they managed to find her. They still haven't lost hope."

"Hope is our daily bread."

"I must apologize. I have to go now. Can I call you again sometime?"

"Of course. Call anytime."

Our girls, our girls, confined in chains, dragging the world along behind them.
Some of them fall to the ground in the water in the dirt in the air on the ground,
leaving the world without meaning, like a clock with only a long hand.
Who's left in the village?

IN THE SABAYA MARKET

When Abdullah told me that he was at the sabaya market last night, I didn't understand what he meant exactly. I wondered if he had really gone there, until he sent me some photos.

"This is a contract from a guy in Daesh advertising a 'girl' for sale in what they call the 'sabaya market,'" he said. "It opens every day at specific times on Telegram, an encrypted messenger. Sometimes a family will find pictures of their daughter on there. Just imagine how that would feel. There might be an announcement for a Quran recitation competition, for example, in which the prize is a young girl. I visit the market once in a while on the chance that I'll recognize somebody."

Abdullah fell silent for a moment. I wondered if he was hoping to find his sister in there?

Then he added, "Just today I was texting with someone from Daesh about the market, and he sent me this photo. He asked for ten thousand dollars."

"I didn't know you were directly in contact with Daeshi."

"I'm not exactly. I'm in touch with the middlemen who buy women from Daesh – not with the intention of marrying them, but to sell them back to their families at inflated prices. Those dealers only pretend to buy the sabaya for themselves. The truth is that they secretly sell them to us. *Real* Daeshis wouldn't allow those girls to be sold outside the country. Anyway, it's less risky for us this way, even if it costs more."

"So who pays for it?"

"We work together to raise the money. The immediate family, relatives, and friends all come together – everyone has a part to play, and needs the others to do the same. You won't find a single family here who hasn't had someone disappear. Everybody's just watching and waiting. Our mountain has melted from the tears and pleas of the families."

"The woman in this photo is wearing modern clothing, not Daesh's Islamic dress," I said.

"Daesh only forces women to wear the hijab when they're outside the house or when an unrelated man comes to visit. But they dress them up in modern clothes, as you can see here, when they're put up for sale or when they're forced into sex. One merchant went into the market and announced that he wanted to see some pictures of girls, and he received dozens of photos of Yazidis. Each woman was posing in front of the camera with a sad expression on her face. The captions underneath read 'Girl #1,' 'Girl #2,' and so on. There's another problem with the clothes, too. Daesh keeps the women and children in the same clothes for the entire duration of their captivity, so that sometimes, if they do make it home, they're still wearing the clothes they had on when they were first kidnapped. Just imagine wearing the same clothes for a whole year, without even having pajamas to change into. A while back, an old woman who escaped all by herself returned to our town, but her entire family had disappeared except for one of her sons. I heard from a relative of mine who went to visit her that apparently she was wearing a dress made out of couch upholstery. And when she was asked about it, the woman explained that she'd worn the same dress the whole time she'd been with Daesh, for more than a year. In fact it was the only thing she wore other than a black hijab that she had to put on whenever a visitor came into her room. She had once been a seamstress – she had other clothes, extra fabric, and a sewing machine – but then she lost everything. She hadn't been able to bring so much as a single needle with her when she was taken. Now that she was back, she couldn't wait any longer. As soon as her son was able to get her a sewing kit she cut a piece of fabric out of the couch and turned it into a new dress. She didn't even wait for the proper fabric to arrive!"

"My God. What about the food? What do Daesh men eat? What about the captives? They have to do all the cooking, right?" I asked.

"According to the accounts of survivors, the Daesh eat rice and soup and meat, while the women eat only rice. Rice every day! The children aren't allowed to eat anything but rice. They're not even given milk, so the captive women grind up the rice and feed it to the children – even those who are still breastfeeding. The strange thing is that a Daeshi believes that any woman he 'buys' actually becomes his wife: a woman who will cook for him and satisfy his sexual needs, both before and after prayer."

"I wonder if the captives who escaped are disgusted by rice now."

"I'd think so. There's an old Yazidi joke about a man who eats eggplant every day – we eat a lot of eggplant, you know. One day his doctor prescribes him some medicine and the patient asks: 'So, do I take it before or after the eggplant?'"

"Eggplant's delicious," I replied, "I love it, but not every day, of course ... Now, here's another picture I got from you, with women dressed in black Daeshi garb."

"That's Parveen, a deaf woman who's here with other captives in a Daesh house. By the way, I just saw Parveen three days ago. I had to work particularly hard to rescue her."

"How did you manage to find her?"

"Do you remember my cousin Nadia?"

"Of course. She's the reason I met you in the first place. When I was trying to get in touch with her you answered the phone instead, and then you helped to translate. That was a stroke of luck."

"I'm also really glad to have gotten to know you – it's really important to me that your book see the light of day so that the whole world will know what's going on here."

"So Nadia was the reason you were able to find Parveen?"

"When Nadia made it out of captivity, she mentioned that there was another woman who couldn't hear or speak who was being held in the same building. Word spread quickly. As I told you, this is a very small town. One day, about three months ago, someone called and told me that the deaf girl sounded like his sister. Nadia's description confirmed it for him. He asked me to do something – to rescue her. That was tough because we didn't expect to be able to get in touch with her over the phone the way we could with the others. Her sister also got in touch. *Parveen doesn't have anyone except for us. Please help us*, she said. I promised to do what I could. The only information I had, which I learned from Nadia, was that she was somewhere near the Tishreen Dam. I sat down to study the map of the region, scrutinizing it building by building: bakery, clinic, grocery store, and so on. My eldest son, Mehdi – he's an engineering student – helped me create a simple spatial plan of the buildings in the area. I let him get involved because I could tell how excited he was to help, and I wanted him to feel this sense of pride, which is unlike anything else in the world. I sent the design to a smuggler whose job was to wander around those buildings, hoping he would see or hear something about a sex slave, a *sabya,* for sale who fit her description, and then buy her. He learned that she had just been sold for fifty bucks to someone from the Hayy al-Jabal neighborhood in Aleppo. She was cheap because of her disability. My hopes were starting to grow. I'd been planning a trip to Syria anyway, to meet up with another smuggler who had helped me out tremendously in setting up a network for rescuing girls. That trip had been postponed for quite a while, but when I heard that Parveen might be in Hayy al-Jabal, I decided to go right away, especially because my friend knew the neighborhood so well. During our con-versation about Parveen and the other women – I'll tell you more about them in a bit – my friend mentioned that he knew a widow who sold boiled broad beans, *baqila,* on the street in that neighborhood. *She's a poor widow with three children. She's clever and resourceful. What do you say we put her on this?* my friend asked. I liked the idea, so we set it up. My friend broached the subject with her, telling her that we were searching for a relative who couldn't speak or hear. We didn't mention that Parveen was a Daesh captive, just that she had amnesia and that we needed to find out where she was. In exchange for walking around with the food cart in Hayy al-Jabal and letting us know if she came across a woman who couldn't hear or speak, we offered to give her a cart filled with a thousand dollars' worth of children's clothing, which was about how much she could make in a year selling *baqila.* The woman accepted our offer, delighted at the prospect of a new cart. Two weeks passed with no information, with no trace of Parveen, but the woman told us that she hadn't visited all the homes in the neighborhood yet, and that she would keep going house to house selling her wares. Two weeks later, the woman had good news for us: *I found her*, she announced. I called Parveen's brother and asked him to provide me with a picture of him with his sister, and another of him opening the door to his car, motioning toward the camera to get in. We made a deal with the *baqila* seller that she would go over to the house where Parveen was being held, and when she found an appropriate moment – that is, as soon as her 'man' wasn't around – she'd show her the photo, and then lead her a hundred yards away from the house, where one of our drivers would be waiting. We paid the woman another installment equivalent to one year's worth of *baqila* sales. She smiled and said, *I know how to get to her. Don't worry.* The woman continued to visit the house where Parveen was being held; finally, when the man was out, the *baqila* seller pulled the photo out from under her clothes and showed it to Parveen. Parveen burst out crying at the sight of her brother and sister. It had been over a year since the Daesh assault on their area in Kocho, when she had been taken away from them. She'd been at her grandmother's house that day to help with housework. Daesh dragged her away from her grandmother and shoved her into a car with other women who were crying. Parveen was silent, as usual, though she wept in her heart. She hadn't seen her grandmother since that day: the last thing she remembered was her melancholy face turning toward her. She had no idea what had happened to her family or to the four chickens she used to take care of. Her life had been so simple, so carefree. She had been able to communicate with other people by signing. On holidays she would dance along with everyone to a beat that she couldn't actually hear; she was moved by the festive clothing and the natural beauty that surrounded their village. But in that Daesh house she could only wear black clothes, just like all the other women who were there with her. The men dressed in all black as well. She had never seen such a colorless world, a world filled with such violence. The man who bought her would beat her whenever she failed to comprehend what he was saying – he didn't use signs the way everyone in her village had. One day he arrived with another man who had just bought her from him. This was how it'd happened every time. By that point she had already been bought and sold ten times, as she explained to us using her fingers. She still had marks all over her body from being beaten by the man who'd bought her most recently. It was his custom, whenever he wanted to have sex with her, to throw some thin cushions on the ground: she learned that this meant she had to take off her clothes and lie down. She would obey in order to avoid his wrath – he would beat her if she even hesitated. But one day when a guest came over, he threw the same cushions down on the ground so that his guest could have a seat. Parveen didn't notice this guest in the room, so she lay down as quickly as she always did. But this time, instead of raping her, he grabbed a wooden cane and beat her until it broke. But finally, one day when he left the house, some woman she didn't know showed up, a woman who was always trying to sell her children's clothes even though she didn't have any children – yet here she was showing her a picture of her brother and sister! Where did she get that photo? And who was this woman gesturing for her to follow her outside?

As if in a trance, Parveen followed the woman holding the photograph. At the end of the street she handed her off to a man standing beside his car waving at her. Parveen was confused but the man quickly showed her a picture of her brother pointing inside the car, and she understood that he wanted her to get in. She obeyed him, obeyed her brother.

"The driver dropped her off at my friend's house, where her brother was able to speak with her through a video app. According to my friend, she seemed to be very happy. She stayed there for three days. Then we moved her to a Yazidi center, where she was received by a woman who took care of her for five days, until they could make it to the Aintab region of Turkey, which is where another friend and I work together to temporarily shelter women before they set out for the outskirts of Zakho in northern Iraq. That friend told me that Parveen was one of the kindest people he ever hosted."

"Amazing work, Abdullah! Thank you so much for calling me back. I have to go meet with students now. Can we talk again on Thursday? I don't have class that day."

"Sure, let's talk then."

Sometimes I get bored of my curriculum so I stop teaching the alphabet and just read the students a poem instead. My students have gotten used to that, which is why, sometimes, if I don't do it on my own, they ask me to read a poem. It's possible they're just being nice. Or maybe they get bored of the lessons. Should I tell them about Parveen, who never spoke with Daesh or heard anything they said, but who learned so much from everything she witnessed?

In a place like that, it must be a great blessing to lose one of your senses, your hearing, for example – just one sense would still be enough to comprehend the scale of the catastrophe, though. After all, violence can hurt without making a sound.

On Thursday, I texted Abdullah to ask if he was available. He told me he was in the car and that he was free.

"But you're driving. Can you talk right now?"

"The best time to talk is when I'm driving."

"I got your message about the little girl who managed to escape all by herself."

"Nazik. She's nine years old. She got away on her own. She didn't call anybody. I'll tell you what happened: She was captured with her mother, her brother, and her sister. Her father was thrown into a giant pit with all those other men who were shot. After nine months of captivity in the town of Naimi, Abu Sayyaf showed up with another Daeshi and told her mother that he'd sold them all except Nazik – she and the two little kids would go with that man from Saudi Arabia, and her eldest daughter Nazik would go with Abu Sayyaf. Her mother lost it when she heard this. She picked up one of her shoes that she'd just taken off by the door and smacked him with it. Abu Sayyaf grabbed his stick and beat her until she collapsed. In the end Abu Sayyaf got rid of the mother and her two children, sending them away with Abu Ammar, who had recently joined Daesh. Like all members of the organization, he soon received proof of ownership of his wife and her property. It doesn't really matter whether or not he manages to claim all of her possessions; the contract between him and the seller applies to whatever he manages to get his hands on. Nazik was left alone with Abu Sayyaf, who claimed that he was going to treat her like his own daughter – but he must have been lying because Daesh marries little girls as young as nine years old. Did you know that?"

"Yes, I did. Just imagine if Daesh actually became a state, with an airport and passports," I said.

"What a disaster."

"It's hard for me to imagine what it would be like as a nine-year-old girl who'd already lost her father, then her mother and her brother and her sister, and then finally finding herself all alone with this terrifying man who just savagely beat up her mother."

"Which is why, as soon as that monster took off, Nazik ran out into the street and kept on running for hours. She had no idea where she was or where she was going. She wandered the streets until it got dark. On some dirt road Nazik saw a sheep. Before she knew it, she sat down on the ground and fell asleep."

In her dream,
she was safe
inside her mother's belly

"When Nazik woke up the next morning, she found herself on a couch in a modest house full of children: two were about the same age as her brother and sister, and there was a little girl not much older than her. They were all awake already, and when she finally got up they were staring at her. After a moment the older girl said to Nazik, *You were sleeping outside our house. We tried to wake you up but you wouldn't move, so Baba carried you inside.* The younger girl ran into the other room, shouting, *Baba! The girl's awake!* A huge man came in to join them. After examining Nazik, he asked, *Where's your family? Are you from around here?* Nazik didn't reply. She broke down into tears. The younger girl came closer and asked, *Why are you crying?* A few minutes later their mother came in carrying a large tray, which she placed on the floor. Nobody went near it; the other children were all glancing back and forth between Nazik and each other. Their mother approached her, saying, *Come on, my child. Have something to eat with us.* But Nazik couldn't hold back her tears, which were streaming down her face even more profusely. The woman took her by the hand and brought her to the bathroom, turning on the faucet. Nazik was refreshed after washing her face. When she got back into the living room, the mother pointed down at the breakfast tray. As soon as Nazik sat down beside it, the rest of the children joined her. The older daughter offered her bread; the mother pushed the bowl of *qaymar* toward Nazik and she smeared some of it on the bread. It'd been a very long time since Nazik had eaten a breakfast like that, but it was the very same food she remembered from back home in Kocho, where there was a woman who would go around to all the houses in the morning calling out, *Qaymar, fresh qaymar!* Nazik's mother would step outside to buy some. The woman would then tip the tray that rested on top of her head over and pour some *qaymar* into her mother's bowl. After breakfast the father repeated his previous question: *Where are you from?* Nazik told them her story in a mixture of Kurdish and Arabic. *Come with me*, the father said. *I have a Kurdish friend. Maybe he can help.* He invited his eldest daughter to come with them. Once the father started driving away, he turned around slightly and said to Nazik, *If someone stops us, we'll tell him you're my daughter.* For three hours they drove down the dirt road and then stopped outside the garage of a house that belonged to his friend, who welcomed them warmly and kissed the father on both cheeks. The man invited them inside, where his wife served everyone tea, which the two men sipped as they chatted with one another.

They both looked at Nazik from time to time. It was clear that they were talking about her. After a while, the father said he had to be going; he and his daughter left, while Nazik would stay with this new family who didn't have any young children, but did have some young adults. They tried to console her by speaking in Kurdish, telling her she wasn't going to be with Daesh anymore. The man asked her if she wanted to go back to Iraq. Nazik nodded. She wanted to go 'home' but she didn't know if anyone was there."

At this point Abdullah said he had to go because he had received a few voice messages. We agreed to pick the conversation back up when he had some time.

Back in Michigan, time was flying. It was after two in the morning and I only had a few hours before I had to go to work. But instead of going to sleep I made some Turkish coffee and sat down to transcribe Nazik's story from the recording I'd made. Sometimes I can't transfer the feelings so I just stare at the walls instead, the walls of a house filled with people who can't be bought or sold – at least that's what we believe.

THROUGH THE EYE OF A NEEDLE

"Would you like to speak with Nazik's father?" Abdullah asked me two days later.

"What do you mean? Nazik's father is alive? Wasn't he among those men who were murdered in the giant pit?"

"He was – but he didn't die. He played dead. He was very badly wounded but managed to survive with someone else's help."

"Did he ever see his daughter Nazik?" I asked

"The Kurdish family took Nazik to Kobani, and from there to Nawruz Camp in Derika Hamko, where hundreds of displaced people lived, including Nazik's uncle. He found her there and then called her father."

"Where is that camp? In Syria?"

"Yes. It's a historical site that dates back to the year 1300 CE. At first it was called Dayr Hammo, which is a Christian name. When the Kurds arrived they changed it to a Kurdish name, making it Derika Hamko, and when the Arabs arrived they changed the name again, this time to al-Qahtaniyah."

"It's more or less the same way Kobani got its name. I looked it up because you mentioned it was a strategic location on the escape routes. I found some interesting information about the origin of the name: it'd been a headquarters for a German company that had won a contract to build the railroad between

Istanbul and Baghdad by way of northern Syria. The inhabitants of the region heard the word "*kumbani*" (that is, company, in English) from the employees. That word started to circulate, then stuck to that area. Over time the name was changed to Kobani. There's another story, though, which claims that there was a spring where Arab herdsmen traveled to water their sheep, and so the Kurds called it Kania Araban, and then the Arabs adopted that name and translated it into Arabic, so they began calling the region Ayn al-Arab, or spring of the Arabs. These days Daesh calls it Ayn al-Islam, spring of Islam."

"Daesh has unleashed a fierce assault on the region, cutting off the heads of Kurdish fighters, besieging the shrine of Sulayman Shah, grandfather of the founder of the Ottoman Empire."

"Have those attacks also affected the human trafficking operations around the region?" I asked.

"Definitely. Smugglers don't pass through there anymore. They use a different route through eastern Syria."

"I wanted to ask you about Nazik's mother, sister, and brother. Have you heard from them?"

"No, not yet. Poor Abu Nazik also lost his mother and his siblings and their families. The only ones left from the extended family are he and his daughter."

"Did you tell me I could speak with him?"

"Yes, but there's only one problem: he's in the refugee camp and only has access to a telephone at certain hours. Because of the time difference it will be four in the morning for you when he'll be able to talk. Or maybe that works?"

"No problem. I can talk to him then. You do that most of the time, too. And besides, it's not a big deal to wake up early once in a while."

"I'll send you his number. His name is Khalid."

I set the alarm for 3:55 a.m., and spent five minutes getting ready to call.

"Hello, Khalid. How are you?"

"Fine, thanks."

"Abdullah told me you were shot at by Daesh."

"They forced us down into a pit and fired at us. They told us in advance that we should get ready because they were going to aim for our heads."

"What were you thinking in that moment? Did anything specific come to mind?"

"Just my family, who were still upstairs."

"Upstairs?"

"Daesh had separated all of our families inside the Kocho school. They took the women and children upstairs and held all the men on the ground floor. There were about four hundred men. They took away our cell phones and whatever was in our pockets."

"Cell phones would come in handy at a time like that."

"The phone's the first thing we thought to take with us when we left the village."

"You left in early August 2014, right?"

"There were maybe two thousand people in a caravan heading into the mountains. I was with my family, my siblings, and their families. We were under siege for two weeks in the mountains; we ran out of food and water. Some of the sick died. Children cried the whole time. A rumor started to spread that there was no longer any danger, that it was time for us to go home, but we didn't know what to do. Then, after a while, once we were on the move, Daesh captured us and made us choose between converting to Islam and going to Zakho, in Kurdistan. We said we'd rather go to Zakho. But when we saw their giant trucks coming we felt like we were still in danger. The men were separated from the women, and they crammed us into about a hundred vehicles. There in the school building, the sheikh's son shouted at them, *You told us you'd take us to the mountains, to Kurdistan! We will,* one of them replied, *but in a little while.* But instead they took us to pits on the farm that were supposed to be our graves."

"Was that farm near the school?"

"About fifty yards away. Sometimes the peasants worked in those agricultural basins, but after the attack the peasants abandoned it and the land dried up. They threw us down there in shifts. Every fifteen minutes they would lower down about a dozen men from the outcropping and open fire on them. They arranged us into rows, telling us to line up next to each other so it would be easier for them to shoot us. My brother was in the first shift. My other brother was in the second shift. I was in the third. I knew everyone down there with me; they were my neighbors and friends. After they shouted *Allahu Akbar,* the sound of gunfire rang out, and once they had finished shooting us one by one, I was swimming in a pool of blood. They shot at us again, then a third time. I shut my eyes and prepared to die, as one must."

"How long did you stay like that?"

"I was bleeding there for almost five hours."

"Where were you shot?"

"In three different places. Once in my foot and twice in my hand."

"And did everyone else die?"

"All except for one other man, Idrees, a childhood friend

of mine. His feet were injured. I tried to drag him out of the pit with me but I couldn't because half my body – the left side – was bleeding. I couldn't lift him with just one hand. *Idrees*, I said to him, *climb up on my back, get on*. But he couldn't move. He was still alive but I wasn't able to save him. I struggled to get out of the pit and walked away from the school. As I crossed the farm road, I heard the nonstop rattle of gunfire, and I dropped down onto the ground, which is where I stayed, hidden under the wheat and barley until the sun went down. When it was finally quiet, I started walking again, stumbling toward Sinjar, making it nearly six miles in the dark. The houses I passed were abandoned, the doors flung wide open, nothing inside but shadows. I almost died of thirst. I'd lost a lot of blood and my foot was so bad I could barely walk. I wanted to rest, even if I had to die right there, but I also wanted to struggle to find out what had happened to my family, to save them from Daesh. Eventually I saw a small ray of light coming from a house in the al-Qabusiyyah area between Sinjar and Kocho. I gathered all of my strength to make it to that house, even if I had to hop on one foot. When I knocked on the door, a middle-aged man opened it. *Can I have some water, please*, I said. He invited me inside. My clothes were covered in blood. He offered me new ones and helped me change. I glanced at the clock on the wall and discovered that it was almost midnight. The man sent his son to a relative's house in the neighborhood to get some grape juice. *You've lost a lot of blood*, he said, *juice will do you good*. I was still bleeding, and my hand had swollen up to the size of a gas can. The pain kept me awake until morning. The man stayed up with me, checking in every half hour, always with a glass of grape juice in his hand. I was there with him for four days – the whole time he went out of his way to care for me. He introduced himself as Abu Ahmad, a Muslim Arab who had always lived among Yazidis. He seemed very sad about what the Muslims who called themselves the Islamic State were doing to us. *Is there anyone else I can help?* he asked. I told him how my injured friend was still out there in the pit. *Well let's go and get him out of there, then*, he said. *Maybe he's still alive. Do you remember where it is exactly? Come on, let's go.* I nodded, but when I tried to get out of bed, I couldn't walk. I fell on the floor. *You need to go to the hospital*, he said. Abu Ahmad called a few friends, and finally he managed to speak with someone in the Peshmerga, who promised to send a volunteer to drive me to a hospital in Zakho. The pickup was scheduled for the ridge at 10 p.m., which was five hours away. I thought that if the car was going in the same direction as the farm, that maybe we could pick up Idrees on the way. Sometimes Idrees would sit next to me at school. He was so innocent; he trusted everyone. Who could have ever imagined that one day we'd be lined up side by side near the same school with people shooting us, as we bled alongside one another, our blood mixing together in a pit? When it got close to 10 p.m., Abu Ahmad carried me on his back and brought me to the ridge, where a car was waiting. The volunteer stepped out and helped Abu Ahmad put me inside. Ahmad gave me his cell phone, saying, *Take this, it might come in handy. Don't worry, I have more.* I asked the volunteer if we could take a detour to see if my friend was still alive. *How long has he been there?* he asked. *Four days*, I said. *That whole area is crawling with Daesh, but we can try, maybe we'll get lucky.* The volunteer turned toward the road leading to the farm but we couldn't find any of the pits. I didn't know what happened. The volunteer kept going around in circles but there wasn't a trace. He tried to steer clear of the scorched fields. I didn't want to insist too strongly so I didn't object when he turned the car around and headed back. I slept on the way, or else lost consciousness, because the next thing I knew I was in the hospital. My surgery took four hours. Afterward I learned that the nerves in my left hand had been severely damaged, that it was completely paralyzed. Thank God, at least I was alive. My eldest daughter Nazik made it back. Now I'm waiting to hear from the rest of my family. We're here at Qadia Camp, in 3,000 military barracks, listening to each other, waiting here for our missing families to come back to us."

"Hello, Abdullah."

"Hi, how are you?"

"Fine. I spoke with Khalid, but the line was cut before I could thank him."

"If you have any more questions, I can ask him for you."

"I want to know more about what's going on in Qadia Camp. Have you been there?"

"Yes. I have a lot of friends and relatives there, so I hear what's good and what's bad with them. I go to a lot of funerals. Death is very present these days, as you know. Imagine a camp full of people when it's very hot and the electricity isn't working. They have generators but half of them are broken. An hour crying. Then an hour laughing. They exchange clichés like: 'I call every day but nobody picks up.' 'Thank God she made it back. I had a feeling she would. First she came back in my dream, then in real life.' 'Have you heard anything?' 'Stay strong. For the children.' 'Oh, please. I just did what I had to do.' 'This bread is for the missing. Take it and think of us.' '*Inshallah*, he'll come back soon.' But the question they ask one another all the time is: 'Who has come back and who hasn't made it back yet?'"

Who has come back and who hasn't made it back yet?

Abdullah began to tell another story.

I met a mother and her children – perhaps you'd like to hear about them. It's about a boy who didn't see his father when he was first born. The boy's father didn't see his father when he was born either. And his grandfather was born without seeing his father either. War swallowed them all up. In the future, when people read stories about them, they might seem like fantastical tales of the djinn, but this is our reality today. It's unreal ...

In the early 1940s, in a village in Sinjar – Khan Sour to be precise – there was a man named Saleh who married a young girl from the village named Zarifa. A month and a half after they'd married a fight broke out between a Yazidi tribe in Khan Sour and the Arab Juhaysh tribe. Nobody knows exactly how the conflict started. As you know, people here have hot tempers, and they'll start fighting at the drop of a hat. Anyway, Saleh was killed in that dispute, leaving Zarifa all alone, one month pregnant. Their son Ali was born – he was raised by his mother. Ali got married in his midthirties, which was considered very late at the time. Zarifa waited impatiently for a grandchild but five years of marriage passed without children. Zarifa would wake up every morning hoping to hear the awaited news. When her patience ran out, she started urging him to remarry – that is, until his wife finally got pregnant; Ali heard about the pregnancy as he was putting on his helmet, in preparation to go to the front – the Iran-Iraq War had broken out and he was called to fight with the other men. Ali arranged for his leave to coincide with the birth of his much-anticipated son, Hasan. But when Ali returned two months before his son's due date, his mother received him by wailing and slapping her cheeks, because he had come back wrapped in the Iraqi flag. They were given a black banner with white letters that read "Ali the Martyr Died Defending the Honor and Dignity of the People." It was to be hung out in front of the house. The three women wore black, in mourning. As Hasan's birth approached, Zarifa picked out a brown dress as a gift for Faheema, telling her, "You can't welcome the birth of your child all dressed in black," but Zarifa didn't change her mourning dress until Hasan turned one year old. The day Hasan was born, Grandma Zarifa held him in her lap, cooing at him in a quavering voice somewhere between a lullaby and weeping: "Your father would be so happy to see you. He was born, like you, right after his father died." And just like Zarifa, Faheema dedicated her life to raising her son, refusing to get married again. When he was in his midtwenties, Hasan married a young lady named Zuhour. The couple had been blessed with two daughters and were then expecting their third child. One day, the two girls were playing hide and seek, and as usual, they wanted their mother to join them, but she didn't because the entire house was in a state of agitation. News had spread that Daesh was moving into the area, which totally confused them. They locked themselves inside their home; they decided to stay there because they didn't own a car, Umm Hasan was sick and unable to walk, and Hasan was concerned about

Zuhour walking long distances now that she was six months pregnant. After two days of self-imprisonment, their food and water ran out. All of the shops were shuttered. Everyone in the area had fled or was getting ready to go. In the end, they decided to do the same – Hasan carried his mother on his back, Zuhour picked up the little girl and took the older girl by the hand. They all headed down in the direction of the village of Kocho.

They joined the hundreds of families who had already arrived – for ten days they were besieged along with the people of Kocho. But then they all fell into the clutches of Daesh. Hasan was separated from his family because "men shouldn't ride on the same bus as women." They separated Umm Hasan from Zuhour and the two girls because "elderly people need special treatment in a cool place." The Daeshis were respectful at first, saying things like "We aren't going to hurt you, we're just helping you get out of here." But everything was set for them to execute their plan. They'd brought large buses, covering the windows with curtains. Even the houses where they took people had been prepared with Daesh waiting inside. The buses headed toward the village of Sawlakh, where they unloaded the women first, detaining them in a large warehouse; the women heard the nonstop sound of gunshots being fired at men who had just been shoved into pits dug for precisely this purpose. After they killed all the men, they took the older women, including Umm Hasan, and threw them into a fishpond. Then they shoveled dirt on top. They buried them alive.

The two little girls clung to their mother in fear, alongside other dazed mothers and daughters. Then they were transported to a prison in Talafar. Two months later, in the same prison, Zuhour felt labor pains – it was time to give birth. Fortunately, one of the captives was a midwife so she was able to help her through a traditional birth. The newborn cried the same way all newborns cry when they are torn from that safe place inside their mothers and brought out into the big scary world. Zuhour was trying to nurse her newborn child when a Daeshi came over and forced them into buses once again. They had sold all of them (three hundred families) to the sabaya market in Raqqa, where they would be auctioned off to Daesh fighters. Zuhour stood in the market, holding her son, with her two daughters standing by her side. A gigantic man, as hideous as a monster, came up to her; she was terrified by the sight of him, afraid he was actually going to buy her. She flailed desperately to mess up her hair and her appearance as much as possible so he wouldn't be attracted to her. Just then another Daeshi, smaller and younger, approached her. She whispered that he should take her. And that's exactly what he did.

Abu Qutayba took them home with him and introduced them to his two wives. All three of them spoke with a Damascus accent. Zuhour was able to guess what they meant. Even though she was exhausted from having just given birth, on top of everything else that had happened to her, Zuhour was forced to wait on them. She would do everything she could for the sake of her children. After two months, she was unable to withstand it anymore and broke down from exhaustion. When she woke up she was still very dizzy, so she sat down and didn't do any of her chores. When Abu Qutayba returned home, his two wives complained that Zuhour was negligent, that she hadn't done any work at all – so he beat her. Zuhour didn't cry.

She maintained her composure so her daughters wouldn't be upset, but her two little girls started crying anyway. As the two wives' complaints about her increased, the beatings continued almost every day, until Abu Qutayba decided to sell her. As the new buyer Abu Sayyaf started haggling over her price, Zuhour hoped that he might be better than Abu Qutayba, that he wouldn't hit her, at least not in front of her children. Zuhour's hope came true in terms of the beatings, but there was a new problem: Abu Sayyaf never fed her. Zuhour would boil bread crumbs in water to make soup for her children. After a month and a half of severe malnourishment, her little boy nearly died of hunger. Zuhour had no choice but to try and escape. She realized that this would be taking a huge risk. She'd heard about entire families who were killed when they tried and failed to get away – roving patrols would bring them back, and these members of the movement had no mercy in their hearts. But because of her baby's screams and the hunger and emaciation of her two daughters, Zuhour wrapped herself in her black abaya and fled with her children the first chance she got. Walking down the street, she noticed a house with an open door. Inside, there was a large sewing machine with a woman standing behind it and five other women sitting nearby. Zuhour entered and sat down with her children. Thinking she was another customer, the seamstress asked her what she could do for her, but Zuhour was too scared to ask for help. What if one of the women ratted on her? "I'm at the end of the line," she told the seamstress. And so the woman took the fabric and the measurements from the other women first.

Just then an armed patrol burst into the room. The women adjusted the abayas covering their heads. Zuhour did the same, as her two girls cowered under her arms. The man excused himself and walked out, muttering, "I beg God's forgiveness."

After about an hour, the seamstress finished her work, and took the payment from the other five women. Only Zuhour and her children were left. The seamstress looked at her, waiting to take her order. Zuhour drew closer, and said, "I'm an Iraqi and I'm at your mercy. I ran away from Daesh. I beg of you, please, give me shelter. That man who was just here is looking for me. If they find me they'll kill me and my children."

The seamstress replied: "Come inside." She opened the door that led from the workshop into the house, then returned to her sewing machine. Before she had finished working on the first dress, the patrol came back and asked, "Where are all the women who were just here?"

"They all left," she replied. "Here's the fabric the six of them left with me."

The seamstress closed up her workshop, which was the front room of her house, separated from the rest of the house by a door and a small hallway. She went inside to check on Zuhour and her children – they were frozen in place on the couch, motionless. She sat down across from them. She told Zuhour, "I would like to help you, but the trouble is that my father is a member of Daesh."

The seamstress remained silent. Zuhour didn't know what to say. Surely she didn't want to wait around for her father to come home. The seamstress clarified: "My father isn't here every day. Ever since he joined Daesh he goes away for three weeks at a time, comes home for just three days, then he goes away again, and so on. You have about a week until my father comes back again. There are two options: either you leave within the week, or you hide out in the storeroom and don't make a sound while you're in there. That room is for my sewing machines. It's my own private space. My father never goes in there."

Zuhour felt profound gratitude toward this young woman who offered to accommodate them despite the danger it presented. Before Zuhour could respond, her son started crying. The seamstress said, "I'm worried the little boy will start crying when my father gets here."

"He's really a very quiet child. He sleeps all the time. But he cries when he's hungry. They didn't bring him any milk when we were with Daesh," she said.

"Let me go buy some milk," the seamstress replied. "Don't open the door, not even if someone knocks. I've got a key. I won't knock. Here's the refrigerator. Eat whatever you feel like. I'll be back in a little while."

Zuhour made some cheese sandwiches, which were particularly good because they were all so hungry. "My stomach was hurting, but I feel better now," the older girl said.

The seamstress came back with packages of powdered milk and a bottle of liquid milk. Zuhour fed her baby, gazing at his content face.

The seamstress introduced herself: "My name's Reem. What's yours?"

"I'm Zuhour. My little girl's name is Reem as well."

"May God protect you. How old is the baby? What's his name?"

"Four months. He doesn't have a name yet. He was born in prison."

"Why were you in prison?"

"I don't know. Daesh attacked us. They separated us from our husbands, thinking we were the spoils of war."

Zuhour shared all the details of her story with Reem. When she started crying, Reem went over to pat her on the shoulder.

"I'll never forget the kindness you've shown us here," Zuhour said, "I pray to God that someday I'll be able to return the favor."

"Don't mention it. I'm not going to let you out of my sight, but I am worried about my father," Reem said, as she gestured for Zuhour to follow her. She showed her the room where they would sleep. Before her father got back, they would pack it with cardboard boxes and supplies, hiding themselves inside so he wouldn't be able to see them. "He never comes into this room. He knows that it's for storing sewing supplies. But we should prepare for the worst," Reem insisted. They seemed tired so she added, "Sleep well."

Zuhour closed the door behind her and hugged her children. The older girl asked, "This isn't Daesh's house, right?"

"No, this isn't Daesh's house. It's Auntie Reem's house," Zuhour said, "but sometimes Daesh comes here. And when they do we have to hide. We can't make a sound."

Zuhour closed her eyes, trying to think of who she could telephone for help – who among them is still alive? Zuhour couldn't remember a single phone number. All those numbers were saved in her cell phone, which they'd taken from her, along with her gold bracelet. She never imagined that she would need to know the numbers by heart. Zuhour couldn't sleep, and the quiet in that house gave her space to think about everything that had happened. Her two daughters had no idea that their father was dead; they thought he was still at home, waiting to see them again. The two girls were very close to him. What would she tell them if they went home and didn't find Hasan there?

The next morning Zuhour slowly cracked open the door, peering through to see if anyone was there. Emerging from their room, she heard the sound of Reem's sewing machine. Zuhour sat down in the living room, which was separated from the sewing room by a small hallway. A little later Reem came in, as if she'd felt Zuhour's presence: "I waited so that we could have breakfast together," she said. "Did you sleep well?"

"We haven't slept that soundly for a long time," Zuhour said.

After breakfast Reem made some Arabic coffee, which the two women drank together. Then the doorbell rang. Zuhour was afraid it might be the patrol returning again. She didn't know what to do. Reem waved for her and the children to go into their room and hide and to lock the door behind them. Twenty minutes later Reem came back: "It's me. Don't be afraid. Open the door. It was a new customer bringing me a bunch of fabric to sew. I just wanted to let you know that everything's fine. I'm going to do some sewing. I'll close the living room door behind me."

When Reem came back from the workshop after four hours of cutting and sewing she discovered that her house was cleaner than usual. Reem thanked Zuhour for that, saying, "You didn't have to bother."

Five days later, Reem was talking on the telephone, and when she hung up, she told Zuhour, "Listen. My father's on his way. He'll be here in about an hour. Come into the store-room, lock the door from inside. We'll have to put some food and milk inside first. You might not be able to come out for three days. Let's pray to God the baby doesn't start crying."

In their hiding place, Zuhour repeated to her daughters that they were not to make a sound. It was so quiet that the two girls fell asleep right where they were. The next day Reem came in and said, "My father went shopping. He'll be back in a little while. You can use the toilet, but hurry."

They all went to the bathroom, then returned and hid behind the boxes that Reem had stacked on top of the supplies, so that they couldn't be seen even if her father went in for some reason.

Those three days passed without incident. Her father left, and wasn't going to return for another three weeks. Zuhour and her children went back into the living room as Reem had invited them to do, and they were able to get back to feeling normal.

The same thing happened three times. Each time he would stay for three days, then leave for three weeks, as if he were on a fixed military rotation. But the third time the baby nearly suffocated when he was about to start crying and Zuhour tried to prevent him by placing her hand over his mouth. He wasn't hungry. He'd just had his milk. But the diapers and the small cloths in the house had all run out, and the baby was filthy. Zuhour tried to soothe him by taking off her stockings and using them to clean him. After sixty-nine days of Reem's hospitality, Zuhour asked, "Do you have a telephone book for Kurdistan? What if we just call some numbers at random? Maybe we'll get ahold of someone who knows me. Who knows?"

Reem dialed a number from the phone book at random. Someone in Sulaymaniyah Province picked up.

"Hello, good evening."

"Good evening."

"There's a woman here with me from Sinjar. She escaped from Daesh and now I'm letting her stay in my house. Would you please search for her family's number and then call me back? Here's my number."

Fifteen minutes later, Zuhour's uncle called Reem and said, "Someone is going to call you right away. He'll tell you what to do."

Reem was surprised that they'd called back so quickly. Zuhour wasn't.

Zuhour's uncle was in the Arbat refugee camp in Sulaymaniyah. As soon as he heard about Zuhour, he contacted me and gave me her number. When I called, Reem answered, and then handed the phone to Zuhour. She explained how much Reem had helped her, how she had shown her the kindest hospitality for two and a half months. She passed the phone to Reem again; I thanked her and said: "I'm going to send a woman the day after tomorrow at eight in the morning. She'll pretend to be a customer. If she tells you she's with Abdullah it means that Zuhour should go with her. Then she'll take her to a taxi that will be waiting for her. I'd like to send you some money as a token of my appreciation."

"Thank you but I don't want anything, just her safety," Reem replied.

Reem felt some sadness about the fact that Zuhour would be leaving soon – she had become accustomed to eating with her and to talking about whatever was on her mind. She'd learned about Iraqi cuisine from Zuhour, and was fond of her children – they called her "Auntie." Zuhour and her children had added a new flavor to her life. Her days were usually measured by the stitches of her sewing machine. On more than one occasion her father had indicated that he wanted to marry her to one of the "heroic" mujahideen. But how would the mujahid treat her if that actually happened? Like a piece of furniture that could break at any moment, the same way her mother had been broken? As far as her father was concerned, Daesh was correct – the world wasn't going to be fixed unless it proceeded according to the path of the Islamic State. He had gone off to fight with them, to enslave female captives like Zuhour.

The female representative showed up right on time. Saying goodbye to Reem with a hug, Zuhour and the children left. "Let me know that you arrive safely, Zuhour," Reem said.

The driver took them to the village of Mas'ade, to one of our safe houses, where they spent a couple of days. From there to Kobani and then to the Iraqi border. I joined them at Arbat Camp because it was an opportunity for me to see Zuhour's uncle, who is a friend of mine. In this camp you can hear all kinds of dialects and languages: Iraqi, Syrian, Kurdish, Turkish, Assyrian, Persian. There are people from many different regions who've taken shelter here: Shabak and Christians who fled from Mosul; Syrians who fled from Kobani; Yazidis who fled from Sinjar; Muslims who fled across the Tigris from al-Anbar on small skiffs. Some children had drowned in the river.

Zuhour told me a great deal about Reem and her generosity, which is why we sent her a gift even before receiving the financial payment from the Office of Kidnapped Affairs. The same woman who'd gone to Reem's house to take Zuhour to the driver went back a second time and placed an envelope in her hand with the word "Thanks" written on it, and a thousand dollars inside. Reem called Zuhour, stunned by the gift. "You should have kept the money for yourself and for your children. You might need it," she said.

"Forget about it. You already spent too much money on us, Reem. I'll never forget the protection you offered us, from your own father even," Zuhour replied.

"I wish I had gone with you," Reem said.

A ray of light passed through the eye of her needle ...

FIVE TRICKS FOR ESCAPING DAESH

"You need tricks," Badia told me when I asked her how she'd managed to escape Daesh.

The first trick was to stop bathing for an entire month, until she smelled so bad that the fighters would stay away from her, refusing to buy her. The second trick was to claim that she was married, and that the little child beside her was her son. It took longer for married women to be sold. The third trick was to pretend she was pregnant in order to avoid being raped, even if only temporarily. The fourth trick was to say that she'd just stepped outside with her girlfriend to get some air – that was the only reason. The fifth trick was to ask permission to call "the American Emir," to make it clear that she was not trying to run away from him.

Badia told me her story: We were a big family living in the village of Kocho – my mother and father, and my five brothers and five sisters. In the beginning we heard that Daesh had occupied Mosul; we heard that they were killing people there, raping women; we heard that they were coming toward us, that they were going to do the same thing to us. We didn't believe it. We traded these stories as if they were straight out of *The Thousand and One Nights*. We heard that they had severe and sullen faces, that they never smiled; we heard that they didn't have mustaches, but long beards. We wondered: Is it true? Are they actually coming? How are they going to get here? Is it true that they are coming with black flags and swords, cutting down anyone who stands in their way? No, that was unthinkable. Daesh was a lie. And even if it wasn't a lie, they would never make it to Kurdistan because the Peshmerga fighters would stop them. We had a hundred soldiers. Surely they would be able to protect us. We shared these rumors until late into the night. At two in the morning my father's telephone rang. It was his friend from the village of Siba Sheikh Khidr. He said: "You have to leave. Daesh has reached our land. They're going to kill us all."

We didn't fall asleep until morning. We would take a few steps toward the door, then retreat. We'd make up our minds to leave, but then remain where we were. The sound of gunfire in the neighborhood grew louder. Meanwhile, conversations swirled among the people of our village and the surrounding villages such as Tal Azir and Karzarak. Finally, a caravan of thirty families emerged and headed toward the mountains. We decided to do the same. We joined our relatives and friends, but just as we were about to leave, a group of Peshmerga fighters arrived, saying they would put Daesh in their crosshairs and stop them in their tracks. Everyone was fired up, including my father. We decided to stay and assist the Peshmerga, or fight alongside them. Then we heard the terrible news that those thirty families that had set out before us had been stopped by Daesh, that they had killed all the men and enslaved the women and children. At that point the Peshmerga made up their minds to go assess the situation and then report back to us. They advised us to stay where we were until they returned with an update. They left and never came back. They didn't send any word. They left us there, adrift. We never learned what happened to them. The only people left in the area were from our village and the village of al-Hatimiyah. Everybody was calling their relatives who had fled, trying to find out whatever they could about what was going on. None of the men picked up their phones. The women who answered their phones said that the men had all been killed. The women had been detained, Daesh had surrounded the area, and it was too late to get away.

At 4 p.m. on August 3, 2014, Daesh came to our homes. Our first shock was seeing men we knew among them. They didn't live far from our village. We even used to consider them friends. But now they had joined the ranks of Daesh. They behaved as if they were our enemies. The *mukhtar* of our village was with us. Abu Hamzah, a Daeshi emir, addressed him: "Raise the white flag and we won't harm you. Hand over your weapons and we'll leave you in peace."

And so they collected all the weapons that could be found in our village and left us there for three days, before returning to the *mukhtar*. Abu Hamzah wasn't with them this time. They told the *mukhtar* that we would all have to become Muslims. The *mukhtar* replied: "We already gave all of our weapons to your Emir Abu Hamzah. And he gave us his word that we'd be safe. Tell him to come here and speak with us." They actually left. Then, Abu Hamzah came just as the *mukhtar* had requested. The *mukhtar* told him: "Didn't you tell us you spoke in the name of Daesh, and that we could stay in our homes in peace if we gave you all of our weapons? Why, then, have these men come and asked us to convert to Islam?" Abu Hamzah replied: "Don't listen to anyone but me. Stay in your homes. You don't have to convert to Islam."

The *mukhtar* took Abu Hamzah at his word. He assured us

that Daesh were gone, that the whole thing was over. But this calm didn't last for more than a day. Abu Hamzah came back with a Yazidi man who'd converted to Islam seven years earlier. Abu Hamzah told the *mukhtar*: "Mr. Kutay here is going to teach you how to be Muslims. What do you say?" The *mukhtar* said they would need some time to think it over. "You have three days," Abu Hamzah replied. "I'll be back on Sunday with Mr. Kutay."

The villagers of al-Hatimiyah heard about this conversation, and they fled the village in secret. Abu Hamzah returned and was angry to discover that the village of al-Hatimiyah had been deserted. He told the *mukhtar*: "I trusted you. Our understanding was that you were all going to remain in your homes. But the people of al-Hatimiyah disappeared. I can't trust you anymore. I'm going to station some guards here. I'll be back in four hours." Meanwhile, tension was growing among the people of Kocho. The *mukhtar* told the guards: "We can't trust you. You tricked us. We don't want to become Muslims."

The guards spread a rumor that a decision had come down from Abu Bakr al-Baghdadi himself that it wasn't obligatory to convert to Islam. Then another group of Daeshis showed up and asked the *mukhtar*: "Are you going to convert to Islam so that you can remain in your homes? Or would you rather leave for Mount Sinjar?" The *mukhtar* replied: "We're going to Sinjar." And the people repeated after him: "Yes, we're going to Mount Sinjar." Then the Daeshi asked: "But why? You'd rather give up your land and your property than become Muslims?"

"We don't need anything. We just want to go," the *mukhtar* said.

"If that's your decision, we'll escort you up to the mountains."

That was 11 a.m. on August 15. About a hundred large trucks and military vehicles were waiting for us. They took us to the school, the only one in Kocho. I was a student there for six years; the school goes from first grade all the way through high school – everyone in Kocho went there. There were two floors. They divided the men from the women and children. Men were on the ground floor, women and children on the second floor.

The *mukhtar* was with us – he was the only man on the second floor. He advised us to hand over all of our belongings to them. We put our telephones and gold and cash into large bags they'd brought. The *mukhtar* told us: "I don't want you to upset them. Give them whatever you have. We just want to go and be rid of them. That's all."

I was on the same floor as my mother and my sisters and my brother's wife. My father and my brothers were on the ground floor. We heard gunshots. We asked the *mukhtar*: "Where are our men?" The *mukhtar* hurried to relay our question to them. They said: "We took your men to the mountains – we were killing all of the dogs. But now it's your turn. Go back down to the first floor now."

We were terrified. The looks on their faces weren't reassuring. We became even more afraid when they bound the *mukhtar*'s hands and put a blindfold over his eyes, taking him God knows where. They didn't answer our questions. They took us to the school in Sawlakh, and separated the unmarried women from the married women. I was the only unmarried woman among my sisters, but I had my three-year-old nephew with me. I told them I was married and that he was my son. My brother, the boy's father, was with the men they had killed; his mother wasn't with us because she had been away in another village with her father when Daesh came. At midnight, all the children who were older than six were taken away from their mothers and sent to a training camp. In the morning they took all the older women, even the pregnant ones, and killed them all. They dumped them into fishponds in the courtyard of the institute, then heaped soil on top so that not a single one of them could possibly survive. My mother was only fifty-seven years old – she wasn't that old.

They brought us inside the school. We didn't know what to do when we heard the gunshots. I knew what was happening – they didn't try to hide what they were doing – but I didn't want to believe it. They admitted that they had killed all those women. Some other women witnessed what had happened, and they told the others. It was the worst day of my life.

That night, they took us to Talafar. I was with my sisters and their children, as well as my sister-in-law and her six children. At the Azahir school in Talafar we met up with the thirty families who had left the village before us. Like us, there weren't any men or older women with them. The exact same thing had happened to them. We all slept on the ground. We didn't have any water. They only brought us a little bit of bread to last the entire day. I had to split a single *sammouna* with my nephew. Some of the women and children died of thirst. At that point a man showed up with a bucket of water. But before we could drink any of it, he threw in a dirty diaper. I don't know why he did this, but we drank the water anyway, despite the filth. We nearly died of thirst. I think they put some kind of chemical in the water because all of us got dizzy and nauseous and tired.

We stayed there for fifteen days, but it felt like fifteen years.

After that they told us: "We're going to take you to another village where you can stay in separate houses, where you can get some rest." They took us to two villages near Talafar: Kasr al-Mihrab and Qazel Qiw. Most of the inhabitants of those villages had been Muslims, but they'd all fled, leaving their homes behind. Daesh occupied them. They took me along with twenty other women to the Kasr al-Mihrab school, where someone they called "the Caliph" came and announced that we would have to marry the fighters.

We said: "We're already married." The Caliph said: "We killed all of your men. So now you're for sale on the market."

A man came into the room, followed by two more men, then five, then even more. All of them were staring at us, smelling us, selecting whom they wanted. There was no use in resisting. Our numbers decreased until there were only ten of us left. They ordered us to bathe, but I went into the bathroom and came back out again without washing. I knew they were going to come and smell me, and cleanliness was dangerous in that situation. A month passed, and every day I began to smell worse. I didn't even wash my face despite the fact that my eyes were itching from crying so much. They brought us fresh clothes to make us more enticing to the customers. They said: "Put on these beautiful clothes. The photographer will be here any minute."

Badia posed with her family for a group photo. The photographer did what he could to include all of the members of the extended family in the picture. Thirty-two people standing in three rows. She was in the middle with her mother and her father and her younger brother and her older sister. The rest of her brothers and sisters along with their families stood behind them and in front of them. The photographer gestured at them to squeeze in closer together so that he wouldn't miss any of them. Finally he took the picture. Then he said: "Wait, don't move, I'll take another one just to be safe."

Badia looked up at the photograph hanging on the wall. She was alone in the picture. Underneath was a telephone number she didn't recognize. She had been told that it was the number of her owner. Anyone could call him and offer a price to buy or rent her.

Badia continued: I hadn't changed my clothes since leaving the village; I didn't go near the clothes they'd brought for us to wear in the pictures.

Then, only seven women were left unsold. Someone came and told us: "Nobody wants you, so we're going to send you to Syria."

They moved us to a building in Raqqa. There I was reunited with my sisters, my brother's wife, and my friends – they said they'd been there for two weeks. After thirteen days they sold us off, ten of us for each man.

An American came and bought me along with nine other women. He took us to his house in Aleppo. His guards there all called him "the American Emir." The first thing he ordered us to do was bathe. He pointed toward the bathroom, saying: "Get in line. Each and every one of you has to take a bath. Or else." Then he brought us new clothes and told us to put them on.

Were they Islamic clothes? Or regular clothes? I asked Badia.

Regular clothes. No hijabs. Islamic clothes were for leaving the house.

Did you wear a hijab when you were in Kocho, before Daesh came?

No. I wasn't veiled. I loved wearing pants. I don't like dresses.

Were there any pants among the clothes the American Emir brought for you?

No, only dresses. I had to wear one. He was very serious about it. He wanted to sell us off as quickly as possible. He said: "I'll keep one of you for myself, and sell the other nine." Then he approached me, and said: "You."

Why did he choose you?

I don't know why. Maybe because I was the youngest?

How old are you, Badia?

Nineteen.

Did he speak Arabic?

He introduced himself to me, and said, in formal Arabic: "I'm an American."

How was his Arabic, in general?

Very poor, and his accent was quite distinctive. Sometimes he would ask one of his guards to translate for him.

Do you know how much the women were bought or sold for?

I've heard five hundred dollars. But I don't know whether that was for one girl or for the whole group. He sold off eight of them. One woman, Nada, remained with me because the buyer refused to take her in the end.

Describe the house for me, Badia.

There was one bedroom for the Emir. I shared another bedroom with my nephew and Nada. There was a living room, a kitchen, a bathroom, and another room for the guards. And there was a room they called the library, where he met with his friends; it contained his personal possessions, his computer, his files, his cell phone, and his TV.

Were there books?

No.

Maybe he meant office, because library and office are very similar words in Arabic.

Maybe.

Were the guards always in the house?

The guards accompanied him wherever he went. But one guard always stayed at the house.

What would he say to you?

During the first three days he didn't say a word. He wouldn't come near us at all. On the fourth night the guard said: "The Emir wishes to invite you to his room." I told Nada: "Come with me." But the guard said: "No, come alone."

He was in the library – or, the office. He invited me to sit down. He said: "I'm going to marry you. You'll become a Muslim, and we'll raise your son together."

With tear-filled eyes, I said: "Why are you doing this to us? Why would you deprive this boy of his father? Why are you marrying married women?"

"Because you aren't going to become a Muslim unless you marry one. Tell me, when was your last period?"

"Why are you asking?"

"Because we don't marry pregnant women."

"It's been five months."

"Well then, I won't marry you today. Tomorrow I'll take you to the doctor to see whether or not you're pregnant."

I went back to our room and Nada looked at me inquisitively. I said: "We've got to get out of here tomorrow. Otherwise the Emir is going to find out I lied, and then he'll rape me." Nada agreed that we would run away the next morning, as soon as the Emir left the house – he went out every day at 10 a.m., and didn't come back until nine at night.

When the Emir left in the morning, we had to figure out what to do about the guard. I told him: "We don't have any bread. We want to buy some." He said: "I'll go get it for you," and he left without locking the door. We made a run for it as soon as he had been gone for a few minutes. But moments later we ran into a group of Daeshis on the street. They said: "Why aren't you dressed properly? Who are you with?" I told them: "With Emir Abu Abdullah the American." They took us back to his house.

We hadn't forgotten about wearing Islamic dress but we couldn't find any in the house. When the Emir got back that evening, he called me into his room. He asked: "Why did you try to run away? Was it because I wanted to marry you?"

"No, we didn't leave with the intention of running away," I said, "we just wanted some fresh air. If we had intended to run away we would have worn Islamic clothes in order to avoid drawing attention to ourselves."

"I'm going to marry you today," he said.

"But I'm pregnant."

"I brought this pregnancy test. Use it now so that we'll know the truth."

Naturally I wasn't surprised when I saw the result. But the Emir was overjoyed, saying: "You're not pregnant. I can marry you today. You'll sleep in my bed tonight."

"But my son is going to wonder where I am. He'll cry if I'm not with him."

"Let the boy sleep with Nada. She'll take care of him tonight."

That night, there was no trick that could save me. He locked the door behind me and forced me to take off my clothes. He started touching me. I tried to stop him. He hit me. I started crying. I pushed back against him instinctively. Like any good woman, no man had ever touched me before. He bound my hands and feet and then raped me. He was surprised to discover that I was a virgin. "You lied to me," he said. "You aren't married. And the boy isn't your son. I'm going to hand him over to the organization."

"He's my brother's son. They killed his father. What was I supposed to do? I feared for his life. I wanted him to stay with me. Please, I won't ask you for anything. Just let the boy stay with me."

"If you want the boy to stay with us, and if you don't want anyone to find out about this secret, you have to do exactly as I tell you." I listened to him in silence, waiting to find out what he was going to ask of me, tears still gushing down my face.

"You will love me. You have to come and ask me to sleep with you, to make love without ropes around your hands or feet."

"I'd like you to do me this favor of letting the boy stay here with me, but is it truly love if it's commanded like this? Is a heart filled with sorrow capable of loving? They killed my mother and all of my brothers in a single day. I don't know where my sisters are. You're an American. You can't know what it means for me to lose my virginity like this."

"I was once an infidel like you. But my life changed when I became a Muslim. I learned the meaning of God."

"But if I'm an infidel, why would you want to touch me?"

"You'll be purified by my touch. You'll go to heaven. My touching you is like a prayer. Something far worse could have happened to you. You could have lost the child. Or you could have been killed for lying."

"I'm already half-dead without my family."

"I also left behind my family and my country. For God."

The Emir showed me photos of his family on his computer: his American wife, his one-year-old son, and his infant daughter. The two children were playing on swings in a park. He said he'd been a teacher in an elementary school.

"Isn't it *haram* for you to abandon two small children who might be wondering where their father is?"

"I go to America every once in a while, to see my family, then I come back."

"I'd like to go to America one day."

"You can go to your room now."

I told Nada everything. She wondered if she was going to be raped, too. I told her: "He didn't say anything about you, but if he does I'll protect you the best that I can. I lost my virginity. That's over and done. I won't be able to keep him off of me now that he found out about the child. But you can still escape."

The next night he drugged me and then raped me five times. When he woke up in the morning, he said: "Don't tell anyone that the boy isn't yours. If the members of the organization find out, they'll kill me. This has to be our secret."

"Whatever you say."

"We'll raise him together, you and I. But I'm going to sell Nada."

"No. Please. I need her. I don't have anyone else. You go to work all day – I can't bear to be here without Nada."

"It isn't right to keep her here – she'll need to be sold or married off. I'll have to marry her if we want her to stay with us."

"No, you already married me. It wouldn't be right for you to marry someone else. I'll do whatever you want."

"If that's your wish, I'll let her stay. She can be our *jariya*, our servant – she can cook and take care of the house."

"Yes, she's our *jariya*."

I went and told Nada that she was now our *jariya*. We laughed about it, and then we cried together. I joked that she would have to obey my orders, since I was "the Emir's wife" and she was our servant.

After living with him for two months we tried to run away, unsuccessfully. We tried to run away four times, but the Daesh police brought us back each time. And each time he punished me with a beating. On the fourth time he was so angry that he strung me up by my feet and beat me mercilessly. Even worse, he left with my nephew, and when he came back the boy wasn't with him. I was beside myself. I begged. I wept. But he didn't care. A week went by and he wouldn't speak to me. He didn't tell me what he had done with my nephew. I went into his room and kissed his feet. I said: "I'm begging you, bring back the boy. Tell me he's alright."

Finally he brought my nephew back. I noticed that the little boy had changed completely since returning. He started asking me to pray and to read the Quran. The strange thing was that he had memorized selections from it. He started reciting them despite his young age. The little boy behaved like a very serious person, as if he were an old man. He acted like a little Daeshi, without the beard. He'd keep saying how much he loved Daesh for no apparent reason. I guess they'd force-fed him their teachings night and day for the entire week he had spent with them. The boy started praying alongside the Emir. Neither one of them knew how to read Quran, though, so they recited the verses they'd memorized by heart. I would pray with them as well, but I wondered when all of that was going to end, when I would be able to regain my freedom.

After my nephew had been taken, we were reluctant to run away again. I was afraid the Emir would take him away and not bring him back this time. But one day an opportunity presented itself that we couldn't pass up. It was 9 p.m. when he called me into his room. He said: "We're going to Kobani to fight. We might be gone four or five days. I'm going to lock the doors. You can't go out – not at all, not even to buy bread. Do you need me to bring you anything before we go?"

"No. We have everything we need. Thanks."

We made a plan to break down the door and run away. We got our Islamic clothes ready and started looking for something to break down the door. We found some small metal tools and used them to smash it. We had to work at that for hours. We didn't go to sleep until we managed to finally break down the door at four o'clock in the morning, but waited until eight so we wouldn't raise any suspicions. We hurried as far away from the house as we could. After about two hundred yards we saw a cell phone shop with a sign that read "International Phone." We went inside. I still remembered the phone number given to me by a woman in that building where we'd been detained before we were sold. She told me: "Memorize this number." Then I gave it to somebody else and told her: "Memorize this number." I repeated the number in my head every day so I would never forget it. We were a few steps away from the phone. I told the shopkeeper that we wanted to use the phone but we didn't have any money. He said: "Sorry. No free calls."

I asked him: "Do you know the Emir Abu Abdullah the

American? I'm his wife. He went to Kobani. I need to call him to make sure he's okay. I'm new here. I don't know anybody else."

He said: "Well, since you're the Emir's wife, go ahead."

After I dialed, a man answered the phone. "It's Badia," I said. "I'm in Aleppo. I need a driver."

Even though I didn't utter the word "escape" because the shopkeeper was standing right next to me, the man on the line understood and asked me for the address.

I asked the shopkeeper's assistant – a little boy – for help with the address, and he picked up the phone and recited it.

Two hours later a driver showed up and asked: "Badia?" We got into the car and took off for another house, where they kept us for two days. Then he gave us a ride to Turkey, and from there to Iraq.

In Turkey the smuggler asked me: "Why are you crying?"

"I don't have anyone left in Iraq. They murdered my entire family."

"You have a brother. He said he'd be waiting for you."

"No, they killed all five of my brothers. They threw them into pits. They killed them all."

"But one of your brothers was only wounded. He's not dead. He managed to get away."

"Which brother?"

"I don't know. I've never met him. But I heard about him from my friend."

I wanted to get there as soon as possible so I could confirm what the smuggler was saying. And as soon as I set foot on Iraqi soil I saw my brother running toward me. We spent a long time holding each other and crying. Khidr was one year younger than me. He's the youngest in the family. I'm the youngest girl.

*   *   *

What about your nephew? Did he make it back to his mother?

Yes. I stayed in touch with him. Later on I asked his mother if the two of them wanted to go to Germany with me, but she refused, saying she didn't want to leave Iraq.

And you went to Germany for medical treatment?

That's right. At first I stayed for nine months with my brother in a refugee camp. As you know, the situation in the camps is very difficult. It isn't comfortable at all. There's a shortage of water and electricity and everything. I left the country with the help of a German organization along with some other women survivors.

Thank you so much, Badia. You're a very brave woman.

IN DAESH'S CAMP

On the Turkish shore,
A calm beautiful graceful child is on his stomach
The wave caresses his tiny corpse
He doesn't seem to protest our ridiculousness,

Though his face is turned away from us,
From our lives overturned like a rusty boat.

The remote control is in your hand. Today you are going to see who will survive the shelling or the flood or the terrorist attack or the new virus. Rowboats rocking in the river carry passengers who left their lives behind, bringing only themselves. But their burdens are heavier than what the boats can bear. For a moment life behind them looks like a lighthouse behind the boats swaying in the river ...

The headline today: Armed Attack on the Turkish Border. Turkish forces attempt to regain control of the borders. Every country has the right to defend its borders. But today I am overcome with extreme anxiety for another woman whom Abdullah had been trying to rescue recently: a mother who got left behind while her infant son managed to cross the border with another woman who was fleeing. Was she trying to cross right when they attacked the border? Three days passed since

Abdullah told me he was able to receive the boy without his mother. "She was exhausted. The other woman had helped by carrying her five-month-old son as they were escaping. When the Turkish border patrol attacked, they all scattered. The mother wound up on the wrong side of the border, while the others managed to get across. I told the other woman that she should stay for a night or two in a safe house, and that hopefully the mother would be able to cross the border and join them," he explained.

I hesitate calling Abdullah again because I'm worried I'll prevent him from taking a call from someone asking for help or someone at the border who just received a survivor. Two more days of waiting before I sent him the text message: *Good morning*, I wrote, then *I mean, good evening*, choosing his time zone. There is a seven-hour time difference between America and Iraq. *Good morning*, he replied, using my time zone. Then he wrote, *Call me if you have time.*

"I'm worried about the mother who was separated from her child. Did you hear anything from her?" I asked.

"No. We're still waiting. But the little boy I told you about made it, the one who was in Daesh's camp. He arrived with his mother and his younger brother."

"They were training to fight, right?"

"Yes. Ragheb was forced to train for four hours every day, learning how to kill, how to chop off people's heads. They would also teach him Quran for two hours a day, and *fiqh* for another hour. They have classes on everything, from how to wash your hands to sex education, from impurity to handling an animal, from genetics to just about anything you can imagine – and things you can't even imagine. And finally a personalized sermon to convince him to die for God, so that he'll be rewarded in heaven. They have special passes to get into heaven that are handed out at the end."

"I wonder what's on those passes? Do they have writing on them? Or a picture? A symbol?"

"He never received the pass because he didn't make it to the final stage."

"That's a shame. So he's not going to get into heaven."

"As you know, they use both carrots and sticks. Their instructions vacillate between brainwashing and promises of a happy afterlife, between death threats and saying, for example, *We'll send you back to your family in a trash bag*. Ragheb was a little boy who'd never even seen a chicken killed before. He'd spent most of his time playing soccer."

"It's horrible to be a girl with Daesh. But it's even worse to be a boy."

"You're right."

"Maybe Ragheb was in school before his imprisonment?"

"Yes, in junior high in Kocho. Our best students are from Kocho. The village is about twenty miles south of Mount Sinjar. Everyone there is related, everyone is very open-minded; they're the kind of people who solve their problems by themselves, they don't wait for solutions from the government. They would personally provide everything that was necessary to the teachers who taught their children. It was rare to hear about a problem in Kocho. Their police were basically out of work. You'd never imagine a major problem like Daesh. Kocho was a place that didn't have any problems."

"I remember you told me that many of the people there didn't leave their houses, or that they went home again after a few hours."

"Yes, which is why so many of them were kidnapped and killed. They never imagined that Daesh would come for them. They'd never experienced evil in their lives. My youngest daughter Rula is six. She asks me if Daesh can get inside our house. When I tell her no, we won't let them, she tells me she's glad to know they're not allowed inside. I buy them lots of toys, no matter how much they cost. When my mother complains about the price, I justify it by saying that it's to make up for how much they suffered during those days in the mountains. My mother chimes in, *Twenty years from now you'll still be giving them things to make up for those days.* My mother is sweet. She makes us laugh, in spite of everything. She tries to hide her tears from us, but I notice them anyway; and I notice the way her ears prick up whenever the telephone rings. Some people tell me that they switch off their telephones when they're relaxing or sleeping, but I can't switch mine off. How would I ever be able to sleep? And even if I did manage to fall asleep, I would be haunted in my dreams. My brother would come striding out of our childhood. I'd see him once again in our garden with our two trees, one beside the other. We used to sit side by side in the shade of the two trees. My father and my uncle had been working together on that garden since the fifties – they'd planted many olive trees. But my brother and I had planted different kinds of trees: mine was a mulberry tree and my brother's was a chinaberry. I'm afraid to go back there one day and see all of those memories. In the old days the people in my village used to plant olive trees despite the fact that olive trees take a long time to bear fruit, sometimes even longer than the life span of the planter. That's why they say 'the olive grower isn't selfish'; whoever plants the tree knows in advance that its yield won't belong to him. Actually I no longer see the point in growing anything, even if it only takes a couple of days, because I can't be sure what's going to happen tomorrow. And I don't like growing a tree that I'll only have to leave behind."

"I know. Abdullah, you left behind your house, your garden, and all of your belongings in Sinjar. If you could be back at your house for one hour, what would you take with you from there?"

"I wouldn't take anything. I'd just want to water the plants, especially the mulberry and chinaberry trees."

After a moment of silence, one of those punctuating moments for which we stand and dedicate to mourning some kind of loss – the loss of a person or a homeland or a meaning – Abdullah returned: Let me complete for you the story of the two boys who were in Daesh's camp. Their father Elias was a soldier in the Peshmerga. He lived in the village with his wife Kamy and their six children, three boys and three girls. Elias decided not to leave the house despite the news that Daesh was coming. After four days, however, his fear for the children grew. Everyone in the area was leaving for the mountains, one caravan after another. They had to travel twenty miles to reach a safe place. Elias and his family walked less than a mile, and then returned home. They went back and forth several times, leaving and then returning, changing their minds about whether to stay in their home or leave it behind. Four days later they left by themselves late at night, walked two miles, arriving in an undeveloped area that was totally deserted. Just then they saw five large transports heading toward Kocho. They rushed to hide in a ditch surrounded by trees, holding each other tight. Elias told them not to move until the vehicles were out of sight. After he had assured them that the vehicles were far enough away they continued walking until they reached the village of al-Masiriyah, between Kocho and the mountain. Some of the people of the village were still there. They were preparing to leave at any moment. They were discussing what to do, discussing what could be done: to flee or to stay. When Elias got there the people crowded around him because he was with the Peshmerga – they thought that maybe he would know more about what was going on than the others. But Elias knew just as little as they did, and in the end they all decided to head west, going around the city and getting to the valley that leads to the mountain road. And that was how Elias and his family wound up as part of a caravan heading in that direction. On the way they were ambushed from the opposite direction by a battalion of Daeshis. They stopped them, asking, "Why are you leaving? Where are you going? You'll die of hunger and thirst. Go back to your homes. Don't worry, we're not going to hurt you. Who told you that? We're here to change your state, not your religion. Tell us what you need and we'll help you. What did you say? A sick person needs blood? Go back home. We'll drive the injured person to the hospital."

At that moment an airplane appeared on the horizon, flying over them. The Daeshis didn't know what to do. They looked seriously confused. They all fell silent. But the plane disappeared, leaving a trail of smoke and disappointment for those people fleeing who had imagined for a moment that the plane had come for them, that it would descend from the sky like a guardian angel. Once the plane had disappeared, one of the Daeshis came closer and asked, "Where is your wounded person? We'll take him to the hospital. We'll give him whatever blood he needs and then we'll bring him home." And they truly did take the sick man with them, gave him some blood, and then brought him back.

The people became even more confused about whether they should keep going or not. They called their friends and families in the neighboring villages and everyone kept repeating, "Don't trust Daesh." They decided once again to keep moving. But this time they would split into two groups. There were about a hundred and seventy people: half of them would walk east, and the other half would walk west. Both routes would eventually lead to Mount Sinjar, the same mountain refuge that had protected them from harm every time. They'd done this many times over the course of history: the people of the region, in times of danger, wouldn't think about going anywhere else, they wouldn't think twice. The boulders of the mountain continued on for fifty miles; it looked unforgiving from the outside but it was womb-like inside. Its passages, like the wrinkles of grandparents, guided the panicked, bringing them solace; its heart was a cave that sheltered the troubled heartbeats of many families, even if at times it silently bore witness to the death of people from hunger and thirst. There was a paved road on which a car would circle the mountain twenty-eight times before reaching its summit. But most went up on foot. A mountain as old as the world – how old is the world, though? Anyway, the half of the caravan heading west reached the mountain, and survived, but the other half heading east, including Elias's family, never made it there. The Daeshis were waiting in their path and they were captured. Daesh took them to Mosul after dividing them into buses according to their gender and age. When they were unloaded in Mosul, Daesh distributed them to different adjacent houses.

The eldest son, Hasan, was with Elias; the two younger boys, Rafeh and Ragheb, were with Kamy; and the three girls – aged eighteen, twenty, and twenty-two years – were taken with the other young ladies to a different house. Through the window of her house Kamy watched Elias and Hasan get killed. She saw with her own eyes how the Daeshis dumped dozens of men into pits, then opened fire on them. Kamy and the other women who witnessed the massacre were all weeping, beating their cheeks the whole time. But the Daeshis didn't care about their broken hearts or their eyes that were reddened with tears. They moved the women again, this time taking them to the Badoush prison between Mosul and Talafar. There, fourteen-year-old Ragheb was separated from Kamy, leaving her with only Rafeh. Nine days later they were moved again from the prison to a school in Talafar. In the schoolyard, adolescent children were forced into military training. Kamy and the other female captives would watch the young men through the window, searching for their sons. Kamy's gaze settled on the face of her son Ragheb – she saw him among dozens of other boys training to fight.

At her home back in the village, Kamy was accustomed to waking up early, opening the window to look over the valleys laid out before her with their vibrant colors that changed with the seasons. But windows had become truly terrifying: through them she had seen her husband and her eldest son being murdered – and now she saw how another son was being trained for violence. He wore camouflaged clothing, a black Daesh flag wrapped around his head. Kamy mustered up the courage to ask one of the Daeshis to bring her son Ragheb to see her. He refused her request: "They went to study Quran," he told her. "He has a sacred mission under the leadership of the Islamic State." Eighteen days later, when Kamy looked through the window, she could no longer pick out her son among the boys training in the courtyard. And she noticed that there were fewer boys in training that morning. Kamy felt nauseous. She wanted to know if her other son was dead as well. Other female captives were also asking about their sons. After the insistent questions, an answer came from one of the Daeshis: "Your sons went to Raqqa to continue their training with expert leaders. Your sons are going to become great mujahideen. Congratulations." Then they moved Kamy and Rafeh and all the other captives to the village of Kasr al-Mihrab, south of Talafar, a village of mostly Shiites who'd left their homes with the coming of Daesh. Now it seemed almost totally desolate. They stayed there for six months, but the number of female captives was declining because they were being sold off. Nobody came near Kamy because she was fifty years old. One day they moved once again, this time to Mosul. Kamy saw a sign that read: *Welcome to Nineveh State.* Before Daesh came it had been called Nineveh Province. Kamy remembered how the people of Nineveh had fled to the northern villages during the 1991 war with Kuwait, and how her house had been filled with people fleeing from the city because of the intense bombardment by coalition fighter jets. Just a little while before Daesh arrived, Elias had been grumbling about how all of the villages in the north had once sheltered those fleeing the war in the cities. But now if those villagers were in danger, the people in the cities wouldn't be able to offer adequate protection. In the end, some of those who came to their homes and ate their food were the same people who'd sold them off to Daesh anyway.

Kamy was craving a cigarette, to inhale some smoke after all her suffering. But smoking was forbidden by Daesh. Nevertheless, Kamy found some cigarette butts in front of the house where she was being held in Mosul. She took them and hid them away. When the Daeshis left, she stood behind the house to smoke those improvised cigarettes. Kamy was startled when a man suddenly jumped out next to her. She saw that it was the water tanker driver, the one who sold water to the Daeshis, and she sighed in relief because she knew him. He spoke kindly to Kamy, in his Mosulli accent, whenever he brought water. He was very nice to her, and he agreed to bring her a new SIM card for the phone that she had hidden under her clothes. Now that he saw her smoking a cigarette butt, he joked with her: "What are you doing? Smoking is forbidden." She asked him if he could bring her some cigarettes the next time he came. "That's really tough," he said, "but I'll try." A week later the Mosulli driver brought Kamy three packs of cigarettes, which she kept carefully hidden. As soon as the Daeshis left, Kamy opened a pack, took pleasure in a kind of luxury, and breathed out some of her repressed anger. She found herself smiling at the generosity shown to her by the Mosulli driver. But the next day she saw something she would never forget: a Daeshi holding up two severed hands in front of the captives. He said those were the hands of the tanker driver who'd brought the captives cigarettes. Kamy nearly choked, as if she had inhaled all of the tobacco of the world in a single moment, thinking, *I wish I were dead, I wish I hadn't asked him for anything.* She couldn't put anything in her mouth for days. Her saliva was terribly bitter. She got rid of the cigarettes, tossing them into the trash and covering them up with other garbage. She decided to never touch a cigarette again.

A few days after this episode they moved again to a camp in Raqqa, where they were put up for sale. Eighteen days passed without anyone volunteering to buy Kamy, despite her cheap price of fifty dollars. She was exhausted from having to clean and cook for a bunch of Daeshis in the camp. Later a wounded fighter named Abu Malik arrived. He'd lost a hand and an eye, so he was compensated with a young female prisoner at half price. And they gave him Kamy for free – she'd heard someone say, "Nobody wants that one. Take her for free." Abu Malik was from Saudi Arabia and he took her and Rafeh and the young Yazidi prisoner to his house in the Tadmur region in Syria. He had four wives living in his house: two were Turkish and the other two were from Syria, but they'd all enlisted with Daesh. Kamy had to take care of them. She did all of the household chores. When she started to get pains in her back from all of the work, the young Yazidi captive offered to help, but Abu Malik warned her that he would beat her if she helped. He said, "That's her job. That's why she's here."

After two months of service, Kamy told Abu Malik, "I want to ask you for something. I have a son named Ragheb. They told me he was taken to a training camp in Raqqa. I haven't seen him since, and I need to know that he's okay." Abu Malik replied, "That training camp isn't far from here. I'll go look for you." Kamy was thrilled. She kept waiting for Abu Malik to tell her that he'd seen Ragheb, but two days passed without hearing anything from him. On the third day she reminded Abu Malik of her request. She continued reminding him every day. On the tenth day Abu Malik returned with Ragheb. He looked at his mother without doing or saying anything. But Kamy hurried over to embrace him and then started crying. Abu Malik said, "Ragheb is training at the Farouq Academy in Raqqa. Soon he'll become a mujahid." Abu Malik didn't let Ragheb stay with her for more than an hour before taking him back to the training camp. Kamy couldn't sleep from then on. The pain in her back had gotten worse – it was unbearable. One day Daeshi fighters came into the house, saying that Abu Malik had been martyred in battle and that the female captives would have to get ready for auction again. This time Kamy's price was higher. Abu Abdullah bought her and her son Rafeh for a hundred and fifty dollars. Abu Abdullah brought the two of them to his house in Aleppo so they could serve him and his three young sabaya. Kamy knew that Abu Abdullah was a director of security for Daesh. She told him, "My son is training at the Farouq Academy in Raqqa. I need to see him." Abu Abdullah promised her he would help. One day he said, "I met Ragheb once. I could tell that he was very smart, which is why I moved him to the security headquarters near me, so that I can train him. He will become a representative I can rely on." Kamy asked if she could visit. Abu Abdullah nodded.

I learned from one of my friends who was a smuggler embedded with Daesh that Kamy and her son were in that house with the rest of the female captives we'd been trying to rescue. My friend would get cell phones to the captives, and we'd make fake IDs for them and provide them with the *niqab*. I made an arrangement with one of my contacts to send a girl to that house, under the pretense that she was selling something, so she could tell Kamy to escape with her. But when she got the opportunity to speak with Kamy about running away, Kamy refused at first, saying, "I've already lost my husband and my eldest son, and my three girls as well. I don't know where they are. Only my youngest son is still with me. I'm not going to leave unless my other son, who's in the training camp, can come with me. He hasn't returned yet, and I don't know when they're going to bring him here so that I can see him. I'll let you know when he gets here. If you're able to come back here, I'll let you know my decision."

When Abu Abdullah got back from work, Kamy asked about Ragheb again. She learned that Rafeh would also need to go to the training camp but that he would be able to come back to the house every day after training. He'd bring Ragheb home every Friday, to bathe before going to the mosque with Rafeh to hear the Friday sermon with the other mujahideen. The sermon lasted for two hours, during which time the two of them would talk about everything, even about how to use the toilet – if you went to the bathroom before prayer was over, your prayer would be ruined. And if you farted – please excuse me – your prayer would be ruined.

On the second Friday, Kamy was finally able to see Ragheb alone. She told him about her idea of running away, her wish for him to join her and his younger brother. But Ragheb refused, saying that he had become a mujahid on the path of God, and that he had a sacred mission ahead of him because God had chosen him among all "the righteous ones." Kamy wiped away the tears and told him that she wouldn't leave without him, and that she would wait until he changed his mind. "Don't forget they're the ones who killed your father and your older brother. Don't forget that, son, don't forget," Kamy said, fighting back tears. "If my father had been on the correct path they would never have killed him," Ragheb replied. "Do you remember your sisters, Ragheb? They raped your three sisters, your sisters I haven't seen since that day. You accept that, Ragheb? Is that the correct path, my son?" Kamy asked. Ragheb lowered his head. It was a perfect opportunity to run away but Ragheb had chosen to go to the mosque with his brother. On Fridays the Daeshis beat any boy over the age of six who didn't go to pray on time – there was a private police force, and their assignment was to beat little boys on Fridays.

Kamy was waiting impatiently for the next Friday so that she could see Ragheb once again. During the day she would pray with Abu Abdullah the way Muslims do, but at night she prayed silently, the way Yazidis do. She concluded her prayer with verses from Allah and from Tawus Malak, hoping that Ragheb would come back to her in body and spirit. On Friday morning Abu Abdullah went to the mosque as usual to meet his mujahideen comrades before prayer. Ragheb and Rafeh would join him after spending some time with their mother. She had washed their Afghan-style clothes so they could wear them to the mosque. Once again Kamy took the opportunity to bring up the subject of running away and returning to Iraq, and once again Ragheb refused. Rafeh listened without saying a word.

Ragheb justified his refusal by saying that his true brothers were those of his faith, which meant that his family was the Islamic State that he defended in the name of truth. And so three weeks passed without her running away, despite the opportunity being there. Ragheb seemed to be completely in step with Daesh: he would wake up early in the morning for dawn prayer, performing his ablutions beforehand, and place a mat on the ground in order to prostrate himself.

When the woman showed up pretending to sell her goods, she threw Kamy an inquisitive look. Kamy whispered that her son hadn't yet agreed to go along with her plan, but that she still hoped to be able to convince him. She begged her to come back again, not to leave her there. On the fifth Friday the miracle that she had been waiting for took place, or maybe some force had answered her prayers. She hadn't spoken with Ragheb at all that day; instead, she was reaching out to him with two tearful eyes. "Why are you crying?" he asked her. She didn't respond at first. Wiping away her tears, she said, "It's nothing, my son. Nothing. I'm just sad." She didn't believe her ears when Ragheb said, "I'm going to come with you."

From that day on, Kamy waited for the traveling saleswoman to return. She looked out the window as usual but she never saw anyone coming but Abu Abdullah. One Saturday three weeks later the woman came back. Kamy greeted her with a sigh, and as soon as they were alone Kamy said that the best time to escape was Friday morning, after Abu Abdullah left for the mosque. He would be gone for two hours, busy with the Friday sermon, and he wouldn't notice if Ragheb and Rafeh were missing. The problem was that the Daesh patrols might notice them because at prayer time they search for the boys who aren't inside the mosque and beat them. But, on Friday, the woman said she could bring girls' clothes with her so that Ragheb and Rafeh could disguise themselves. Then she would guide them to the safe house where they would hide until the driver could take them to the border. Sleep hadn't come easy for Kamy since she'd been taken captive, and it certainly wouldn't be easy that following Thursday. She stayed awake until Friday morning when the plan was carried out. Everything went exactly as she hoped it would go, even if she suffered a bit when she tried to convince Ragheb to put the girls' clothes on over his own – he refused at first but she begged him, "You're going to put us in danger. Just think of them as security clothes. You can take them off as soon as we're out of harm's way." The second obstacle was that they had to spend seven days at the Turkish border without shelter and barely any food. The smuggler came every day and joined them in their attempt to cross the border, but the police would spot them on the road and they would have to go back into the wilderness once again. In the few moments when the coast was clear, their car sped toward the Ibrahim Khalil border crossing, then they were able to turn off the road and walk along the ridge, within view of more familiar territory …

When I met Kamy I was moved by how she expressed her feeling of gratitude. She made me laugh when she said, "I could carry you and your car with my gratitude." I noticed that she was holding a very large cup of tea, and I said, "Seems like you really like tea." She replied that she can't get enough tea. During the week that she spent out in the wilderness along the Turkish border she was desperate for tea. "A cup of tea is all I wanted that whole week," she said.

THE EXODUS

Like the turtle,
I walk everywhere
with my home on my back

I was in an airplane flying from Detroit to Pittsburgh, where I would do a poetry reading at the City of Asylum tent and give a workshop at the Carnegie Museum of Art in conjunction with the *She Who Tells a Story* photo exhibition. As soon as I landed, I saw that I'd missed a call from Abdullah during the flight. But I learned that he was going to be unreachable for a while because of some complicated rescue operations in Syria.

In Pittsburgh, Diane and her husband, Henry, who founded the City of Asylum project, took me on a tour of houses that had been turned into works of art by asylum seekers. Artists painted on the walls, writers wrote words on the doors, and musicians greeted visitors with their songs. But what fascinated me the most was the garden, not only because the residents had planted their favorite varieties, but people passing by had written down their dreams on pieces of paper that were clipped to the fence. The following day, I thought of those dreams that hung like laundry on the line as I contemplated the photos of the *She Who Tells a Story* exhibition, which included works by women from Iran and the Arab world. *Today's Life and War* was a photo of an Iranian couple hanging their laundry on barbed wire – their pieces of clothing looked like white flags in a time of war, or like delayed dreams.

For eight years, we were busy killing them, and they were busy killing us. That was enough time for the dreams, theirs and ours, to dry on the ropes.

Another picture I paused in front of was *Aerial I*, from *Shadow Sites II*. It reminded me of the 1991 Gulf War, when the satellites took pictures of us from above, and we appeared merely as dots moving in various directions – you couldn't see the fear that was the cause of our random movement. Being unable to go to the bathroom, for example, because we were walking in the open air – like everyone else who'd escaped the war – was not something shown in the images taken from above.

The satellite images depicted us as rows of ants leaving their hills, leaving behind everything they had worked at for their entire lives. Every passage was an exodus for them. Our houses looked like dark holes, sometimes lit by the explosions.

My home was in that little spot right there. Can you see it?

From above, it isn't possible to see inside the houses, to recognize the lives of the inhabitants, their struggles over the little things and the big things, their movements getting slower and slower all the time. From above, the burnt fields and bewildered animals look more like an abstraction.

From above, there are no souls, only bodies, but they are seen as hollow forms, moving the way atoms do in the universe – unseen. From above, it's possible for bodies to disappear, to assimilate into water or earth or fire or air.

The signs on the paths reflect the loss of souls or bodies or both. From above, bodies intersect in lines and squares and circles – they look like scars on the face of the earth.

From above, forms are shadows of reality, like those in Plato's Cave.

To see those intersecting dots and lines is to find myself back in Baghdad: here, we are moving out of our house. My mother seems concerned about the heavy stuff we can't carry with us – the Persian carpet, the piano, the antique sewing machine.

The mirror on the wall
doesn't show any of the faces
that used to pass
in front of it.

In action movies, fires are started, walls crumble down all at once, planets shake, birds fly off the trees. But we weren't in a movie when we saw all that happen. This was our reality.

As if I can smell the hospital …

The fragments of my memory interact like fish swimming without running into one another. The scenes don't necessarily proceed according to logical or chronological order, displaced as if they are clips spliced together from unrelated films. I don't know, for example, how a memory of when I entered the men-only Hassan Ajmi Coffeehouse with some male poets is crammed in with the memory of my middle school history teacher's table that had a broken leg. I never liked that book full of invasions or the pictures of "heroes," but my teacher warned us not to complain – "Complaining is the Devil's work." The memory of a Friday trip to the amusement park is always linked with the song "You Are My Life," but this makes sense because that song was playing while we were on the Ferris wheel, where the heartbeats rose as the wheel turned with the powerful voice of Umm Kulthum. I don't know why I remember that dress I hated wearing because it was so fancy and uncomfortable. I was forced to wear it for my tenth birthday. The banned books wearing the covers of unbanned books in the Mutanabbi Street book market ... the boiled chickpeas with bitter orange in the vendors' carts ...

I could never understand how the birds remembered their old songs!

I don't know how to reconnect with that world that has receded fifty years behind me into the past: my father carries me on his shoulders through the streets of Baghdad. He stops every once in a while to buy me something, or to greet someone he knows, or to check the titles of the movies coming soon to the cinema. My father died due to a lack of treatment in the hospital. The hospital was only rooms filled with beds – it contained sick people but didn't cure them. "Lives are in God's hands," they always say. But a drunk once said, "Lives used to be in God's hands. Now they're in the hands of whoever."

The dead
act like the moon:
they leave the earth behind
and move away

The boy next door – who used to play in the street with my brothers, who greeted me with a wave but never said a word to me – left wearing khaki and boots, lifting his helmet slightly in a simple greeting, saying nothing. He is the one whose name was written in white letters on that black banner in front of their house, so his mother could be called the mother of the martyr instead of the mother of Tawfiq.

Forgotten
the faces of the dead
as if we met them once
through revolving doors

I was in a ship on the Tigris when I wrote my first poem. I gave it to my cousin and he made it into a paper boat. He tossed it into the river and we watched the boat-poem drift away down the river.

My paper boat that drifted into the river
with the world behind it
had a special note.
It may arrive one day
although late
all truths come late

One day, in the kitchen, my period came. I told my mother and she said, "All girls bleed!" *Really?* I wondered, *It's scary that we have to bleed every month*.

Two years later, in that same setting, I heard my mother tell her friend, "Did you hear the news? They're sending all the boys to the front to fight the Iranians."

When her friend left, I asked my mother, "Are they going to send the girls, too?"

I thanked God for being born a girl. Who knows how much

the boys were going to bleed over there – they could probably bleed anytime, any day of the month, unexpectedly, maybe without any treatment.

A siren went off and the lights went out. We were instructed to turn off the lights every time we heard the siren. That's why I came to believe that the war was a button to turn off the lights.

Someone drew a circle in the air, but half of it disappeared. Each of us tried to complete the circle. We called it the moon, but it wasn't. We called it the globe, but it wasn't ... Each of us brought a word to call the circle. Our words are half the story. Nobody knows the whole story.

Which side of the circle
is your story?

The war that was born with us is the same one that played hide-and-seek, the same one that survived alongside us, the same one that is growing older with us. I was supposed to postpone my plans to leave Iraq for a week so that I could attend my brother's wedding, but he said, "Who knows what might happen tomorrow. We'll send you the video later."

Oh, little ants
how you move forward
without looking back.
If I could only borrow your steps
for five minutes.

Only a few friends knew I was leaving the country. "Where do you want to go? America?" one of them said. "But don't forget, poetry only exists in the margins over there." For that friend, nothing could be worse than marginalizing poetry! When you live for words, they may actually end up costing you your life. I wasn't sure if my friend had been at that strange meeting at the Hall of Celebrations I attended a month before leaving the country. Maybe he wasn't there. But he was a journalist like me and that meeting was obligatory for all journalists in Baghdad. I don't recall seeing him. But how would I have seen him? How would I see anybody? We were all turned into sheep with exactly the same horns. How should I be able to recognize any of us? There was no way to tell who had thrown trash at the editors on stage. No way to know who hit them with the butts of their guns. No way to know who shouted out the word "traitors." No way to know whose blood was all over the stage. It was the same stage where Shakespeare's plays had been performed by actors who killed one another in the same way, but the difference was that at the end of the play the actors would hold each other's hands and take their bow for us, as we the audience would applaud for them. The curtain would be lowered in front of them, but we would know they were still there, and that their disappearance wasn't forever.

All of us are autumn leaves
ready to fall at any time.

These days, people are leaving the homeland without suit-cases. I was lucky because I left with one.

My suitcase was my time capsule: I filled it with handwritten letters, poems (including some that were unsuitable for publi-cation), drafts of novels by my friend Lutfiya al-Dulaimi (she was about to throw them in the trash), a silver flower that was a gift from a friend in Tunis (he said its fragrance is eternal), another dried flower inside my copy of *The Little Prince*. I left behind hundreds of books with a relative who said he would store them in his warehouse until I came back. Two years later, when I arrived in Detroit, he called me to apologize because he had to tear up the books in order to wrap the sandwiches at his restaurant on al-Rasheed Street. The sanctions on Iraq made everything smaller: papers and bread and hopes. I don't think he would've been able to use the little poetry book by my friend Abdul Ameer Jaras – that book was smaller than any sandwich. It was as small as a book of matches.

Because I had to leave in a hurry, I couldn't find the book I wanted to take with me. It was called *The Elephants Graveyard*, which was about the habits of elephants, the way they live and die. It used to be my favorite book. When a group of elephants faces danger (usually when humans are hunting them for their ivory), the rest of the elephants will leave the area in protest. The elephants that live together also die together, so they go to the graveyard together and lie down there quietly, as if they had just finished some long and exhausting work.

We weren't elephants, so we didn't do any such thing when "the others" left the country. Every time they leave, and we stay.

During the Iraq–Iran war, the Iranians were forced to leave Iraq because they were "enemies." My friend Amani was one of those "enemies." She was studying with me at the University of Baghdad. She and I both loved to walk along al-Nahr Street, and sometimes she would stop by the vendors to buy turnip cooked with date syrup. Amani was going to marry a high-ranking officer in the military so that she could be exempted from the order to leave the country. She didn't love or hate this man, but she loved Baghdad and wanted to stay even if her parents had to leave. In the end, the officer couldn't marry Amani – the government didn't give him permission to marry a woman who was "affiliated" with Iran. She told me this as we marched together in a student demonstration we attended without knowing why exactly. Deep down inside, I felt I was marching to protest Amani and her parents being forced to leave Iraq. I didn't know what to tell her so I teased her, "Amani, my enemy friend."

Thirty years before Amani's departure, my grandmother's best friend Salima was forced to leave the country with all the other Iraqi Jews, following the *Farhud*, when their houses were pillaged and some of them were murdered. "She used to come to all our weddings and funerals," my grandmother said, "and we used to celebrate both of our holidays. I taught her how to make *klecha* dessert and she taught me how to make *amba* pickles."

MY GRANDMOTHER'S GRAVE

Pythagoras once said, "Beans have a soul," and therefore we shouldn't eat them. But my grandmother said the opposite – we must eat beans because "everyone who eats beans goes to heaven." There's another difference between Pythagoras and my grandmother: numbers for my grandmother had only one task, to count the days between the visits to see her daughters; numbers for Pythagoras meant the world. My grandmother had ten daughters and she would visit them in turn, leaving exactly the same number of days between each visit. If she was late to visit one of her daughters, she would delay the next visit to the other one. When she took me with her, she would sit me on her lap and wrap me up with the edges of her long and wide black robe. I never saw her wearing colors or any other style of clothing. She told me those were her clothes for mourning her daughter (my eldest aunt), and that it would have to accompany her to the grave.

Like a baby kangaroo inside her pouch, I would turn my head toward whoever was speaking, and when I got bored, I'd pull the edge of her robe to cover my head with it. She would pull it back, and I'd cover my eyes with my hands. "When are we leaving?" I'd ask her. I couldn't wait for the bedtime stories she would tell me when we went to sleep on the roof of our house. Every night she told me animal tales with a moral at the end of the story. I wanted to have that book, to read it by myself and look at the pictures, but she would always repeat, "There is no book. These are stories we pass down from generation to generation." I would fall asleep to her voice, and the animals would come, sometimes in different roles – the ant might leave behind her grains that she should have stored for winter, and hang out with the grasshopper in the fields instead. In the morning I would be awoken by flies and the blaring sun; I would go downstairs to write the stories down in my notebook and draw them however I wished.

When I got a little older, my grandmother switched to real stories, about how she got married when she was fourteen, how she thought her parents had abandoned her, giving her so suddenly to a stranger: "He was a very kind man, but he barely talked to me," she said, "and when he went to sleep, he covered his eyes with a handkerchief."

The first time I noticed that my grandmother was losing her memory was when her relatives came to offer their condolences for the death of her brother. She seemed surprised by the news with every new guest – she was sad over and over again. Her memory loss started with the death of my grandfather. He died so quietly, as if he didn't want to bother anybody. He appeared to be napping. But he was taking longer than usual to wake up that time. The same day we were busy with my brother's accident. A car had hit him as he was on his way home from school. My grandfather first heard about it from an eyewitness, who said that my brother wasn't moving after the accident. That news killed my grandfather, according to my grandmother. "I know him, he keeps it all in his heart," she said, "he died from shock, nothing else."

At times my grandmother talked to herself, in some kind

of soliloquy, as if she were praying, repeating the same prayer over and over, something like those Sufi circles when they whirl and whirl until they give the bystanders a headache. I followed her gaze, and I saw a sparrow sitting on a branch. Was she talking to the bird or to God? Suddenly she noticed me there next to her, and she talked to me about the houses in our neighborhood, but she switched the names of our neighbors with people from her old village. She put her clothes in a bundle, saying she was going to her parents' house. One time, she sleepwalked and almost fell off the roof of our house. My mother ran over and pulled her back at the last minute. After that incident, we stopped sleeping on the roof. Anyway, the war started around that time and most Iraqis stopped sleeping on their roofs as well – suddenly, sleeping without a ceiling seemed unsafe. The sky above seemed barren and blemished, now that it was dotted with missiles and airplanes that sometimes dropped spent bullets onto our roof. We would find the cartridges when we went up to hang our laundry. After all, our parents didn't allow us to count the stars on our fingers because those stars we counted would appear in the morning on our fingers as boils. Who knew what would happen if we counted those bullet cartridges, or if we went beyond that and dared to count the bones in the mass graves.

War for my grandmother was always "the world war." I wasn't sure whether she meant World War One or World War Two. She wouldn't specify, and even though those two wars didn't take place in Iraq, my grandmother knew a lot about them. The first took place early in her life, the second happened in the middle. But this new, local one, which happened late in her life, seemed to abolish the divisions of time in her memory, so that the events and the details got mixed up. Her speeches about food shortages, in which "people eat each other even as they extended their hands to help one another," was straight out of World War One. But after the second Iranian bombardment, she would ask about her friend Salima, saying that she left her house empty-handed – and that's from World War Two. I tried to arrive at an understanding of what she meant, as if I were holding onto the line of a kite being pushed farther and farther in another direction by the wind.

My kite finally settled down on a tree branch, on a meaning: war comes with various names but with only one face.

"Salima didn't leave by choice," my grandmother said. "She would never leave her home."

"Who made her go?" I asked.

"I don't know, the merciless ones," she replied.

My grandmother could never imagine that the merciless ones would destroy her own grave. They did that in 2014 in the northern Iraqi cities and villages – they destroyed all the graves with Aramaic and Hebrew writings engraved on them:

When my grandmother died
I thought, "She can't die again."
Everything in her life
happened once and forever:
her bed on our roof,
the battles of good and evil in her tales,
her black clothes,
her mourning for her daughter who
"was killed by headaches,"
the rosary beads and her murmur,
"Forgive us our sins,"
her empty Ottoman vase,

her braid, each hair a history –

First were the Sumerians,
their dreams inscribed on clay tablets.
They drew palms, dates ripened before their sorrows.
They drew an eye to chase evil
away from their city.
They drew circles and prayed for them:
a drop of water
a sun
a moon
a wheel spinning faster than the Earth.
They begged: "Oh gods, don't die and leave us alone."

Over the tower of Babel,
light is exile,
blurred,
its codes crumbs of songs
left over for the birds.

More naked emperors
passed by the Tigris
and more ships ...
The river full
of crowns
helmets
books
dead fish,
and on the Euphrates corpse-lilies floating.

Every minute a new hole in the hull of the ship.

The clouds descended upon us
war by war,
picked up our years,
our hanging gardens,
and flew away like storks.

We said there isn't any worse to come

Then the barbarians came
to the mother of two springs.
They broke my grandmother's grave: my clay tablet.
They smashed the winged bulls whose eyes
were sunflowers
wide open
watching the fragments of our first dreams
for a lifetime.
My hand on the map
as if on an old scar.

The "bundle" that my grandmother left behind in her room on the first floor of our house contained a wooden comb, a hand fan, and Turkish coffee cups that were mementos from her friend Salima. What the dead leave behind is a personal archaeology. There's some history in that, a memory of an absence that lasts longer than a day and a night, an absence that lasts many days and nights, days and nights. Their fingerprints on the doorknobs, their fingerprints on those little things like a watch that can tell you the time but can't tell you when her time was up, when her heart stopped – what time it was when it didn't matter anymore what time it was.

Is that why they exhibit personal effects in museums? Isn't it an attempt to give form to sorrow, so that the viewer can take comfort in her submission to the form rather than having to think about the actions that led to it? We attend to the traces of life because we want to participate in that life – and to see a trace of ourselves in it – don't we?

In the September 11 Memorial and Museum in New York, for example, there's an unbearable exhibition of slices of life, broken in the middle of their flow, a warehouse of disappearance that is deafeningly silent. The pictures of people in one album are just a part of an infinite number, if we think of the endless stories behind each picture.

On the shelves of souvenirs in the gift shop, one can buy the past – the past in fragments.

Among the artifacts that were scattered from the two towers: a card of new year wishes, keys, individual shoes, a tissue box, cell phones, construction project drafts, photos of loved ones, business cards, wallets, a hat, a ring, a bag, an empty envelope that used to contain a message, we don't know what or for whom, airplane debris, and a rake that was used to search for human remains.

In the year after the fall of the two towers, a marble statue of Adam fell to the floor of the Metropolitan Museum in New York; it fell for no reason, and smashed into hundreds of pieces. A team of specialists worked for a decade on the broken Adam – six feet, three inches of him, carved during the Renaissance by Tullio Lombardo – until they were able to restore it and get him back up on his feet again.

Several months after Adam's resurrection, a group from Daesh destroyed several monuments in Mosul and Nimrod in northern Iraq. I saw the stones being ripped apart from one another after having been connected for thousands of years.

After the first minute of this video made by Daesh, I said to myself, "Maybe we can restore these statues as well." But in the next minute, the terrorist took out a hammer and started smashing the pieces into smaller and smaller fragments. My hope, similarly, was becoming smaller. I nearly lost my temper – I wanted to break my plate over the head of that Daeshi as he was going after every last piece, crashing loudly as they fell onto the floor. But I didn't scream and neither did the statues. Their brokenness was hidden under layers of stone and history, just as our brokenness is hidden under our skin.

"Let the statues be sacrificed for the people. We don't care about them anymore. Our people are being killed in front of our very eyes," someone commented on Facebook.

"But they're eliminating our monuments, erasing them from existence. They destroyed our houses and now they're destroying our historical houses," another Iraqi replied. But the post that attracted my attention on Facebook that day was a picture of an Iraqi shop with a sign in front that read, "Please don't bomb here. More than half of the items are on loan. Thank you." The next post was a photo of Mutanabbi Street in Baghdad – books were laid out on the floor after its reconstruction. Some years ago, a car bomb exploded, scattering books and bodies, and damaging cafés all along the street. We probably needed to put up a sign that said, "Please don't bomb here. There are still books to read."

THE CHIRP

Amid news of explosions, conflicts, and viruses, a team of scientists found a "chirp" belonging to the beginning of the world – and it was brought to our current moment. A chirp, like God, both far away and close at hand, or maybe this majestic and delicate chirp is the very word of God?

It's said that when we sleep at night, He speaks, and the stars exchange His words as secrets, and we see them as orbits without being able to hear them. But today, God finally spoke in broad daylight, from that far corner of the universe, as a chirp. We can hear it clearly, the way we hear a bird on the tree outside of our house.

I wonder why He broke His silence – maybe He can't stand the misdeeds of humans against themselves anymore, especially those that are committed in His name.

Otherwise, what's the meaning of this sign that He sent us after 200,000 years of silence?

When someone waves his or her hand, the world responds to that wave at the speed of light; the world expands a little, according to the theory of relativity discovered by Einstein a hundred years ago. Then maybe the world, by the same logic, becomes narrower when someone offends someone else. It would become much narrower when the offense is rape or murder, for example. Maybe the universe is now squeezed so tightly that even God can't stretch His legs; maybe He can't breathe and finally had to let that chirp out of His chest.

Maybe He's about to tell us a new tale! A magnificent tale to distract us from all the violence, the way Scheherazade did for Shahriyar.

Or maybe it's just a drop of rain tapping on the roof of an empty house?

Or an echo? (In empty houses, it's easier to hear the echo of absence.)

Or a step? (Are there any footsteps tonight?)

I look out the window and see the trees lined up next to one another, some are almost totally dry, in need of water, their remaining leaves still waving at the passersby, especially the lonely ones whose loneliness is ripening before their very eyes. Trees don't ask why they don't move from place to place, nor do they ask any other meaningless questions. But their branches tremble when the birds leave them, just as the soul trembles when loved ones depart.

I don't know if our dreams are reflections of reality, or if reality is a reflection of our dreams. In one of my dreams, I went back to Uruk and wrote on clay tablets, from right to left, then from left to right. I drew squares, triangles, and circles to indicate the homes I'd had, the stuff I'd owned, and dead people I'd known. Gilgamesh came and gave me the plant of immortality, but it disappeared in a second. I don't know where it went. Gilgamesh seemed so sad, and I concluded he was still in mourning for his friend Enkidu. I wanted to console him but I didn't say anything – it seemed as if he wanted to console me, too, but he didn't say anything either.

In another dream, I found myself face to face with Pluto. The planet had a crack in its face like a mouth, from which words would pour out into space: Hey, sons of earth, why did you abandon me all those years as if I were an unwanted child? And just because I was different, because you couldn't see me, you decided I was dead. I wasn't even asleep.

There weren't any borders in the universe between the planets, so it was simple to travel to any of them. I wanted to go and see if there were really other creatures. Would they know that we exist? Do they have any idea about our planet Earth? Would we be embarrassed if they discovered us and saw all our flaws? Maybe they'd be surprised by our sometimes crazy behavior. Maybe they'd love us because of our vulnerability. Maybe they'd get scared of our dangerous lives. What are their lives like, anyway?

I don't know the name of the planet I visited, but I kept looking back at Earth because I didn't want to get lost. My heart beat loudly as I looked at its spots, both dark and light. I was worried to be so far from the sphere that was my home – not a specific home, since I've moved from place to place and can't tell which one to call home and which one to call exile. In fact, I don't really care. The spider makes a home outside of itself – it doesn't know the difference between home and exile.

The Earth moved farther away, and I didn't know whether to stay close to it or move farther away and discover those other creatures. All the familiar creatures I know and love so well, despite everything, are there on Earth. I'm afraid of getting too lost. After all, I'm not a pigeon and I don't know the way home.

I was alone in the galaxy. Then a woman came up to me. I knew her right away. It was Enheduanna, history's first poet. What was Enheduanna doing here? Maybe she'd had the same question about me. Maybe whoever said that poets

are like astronomers – never getting bored of examining the
little things – was right: that tiny blotch in the Milky Way, for
example, or the shadow cast by the movement of the planets.
They wouldn't mind spending a light-year to see something
new on the horizon, the way a new email pops onto the screen.

Enheduana said, "I'm from Iraq."

"Me, too."

"I'm the eldest of five kids, the only girl."

"Me, too."

"I was my father's favorite."

"Me, too."

Then Enheduanna was silent, so I said, "I read your poems
in praise of Inanna. Was she your favorite goddess?"

"In the lands of Sumer, we had freedom of worship, so we
sang to any god or goddess we loved. What about you? To
whom do you sing?"

"Nisaba, the goddess of writing," I said.

How shall I call you
when you have ninety nine names?

I say "Nisaba"
and I mean praises for the little things,
I mean the big things,
I mean the little things with their big shadows:

the number to round
off the casualties to zero;

the chalk
in the hand of a girl

who draws for the world,
a circle with everyone inside;
the wings open
over the flames;

the soft moss
visible, briefly,
through the river
like the faces of the absent ones;

the comma between
death and life;

the everyday practice
of the doctor
with the stethoscope
pressed against the chest;

the blue flower
in Novalis's dream.

My dreams are strange. I was with Enheduanna, and then I found myself with Siri. She emerged suddenly from my phone, like a djinn who would grant me all of my wishes. I wasn't surprised to see her in human form, and not merely as a sound. I asked her how she was. "Fine," she said, "except that I dream of leaving my job as a robot." She didn't want to react in such a professional way each time someone summoned her. She dreamed of getting out of that prison – going to the gym or having a nice meal; she dreamed of combing her hair, of growing her hair long, having a house and being able to have company over, of expressing her opinions freely, of finding ears that would listen attentively to her – like the ears of the blind. She dreamed of having her questions answered as well.

My dreams are probably the result of the stories I'm living through these days. I find myself kidnapped by strange creatures from outer space. I try to run away but I can't move. I say, "I'll be going now," but I can't move, as if I'm one of Samuel Beckett's characters in *Waiting for Godot*.

Finally, I find myself coming back to my country. Abdullah is at the border to receive me, dressed all in white. He says, "You came back, finally."

His words were still buzzing in my ears: a woman was crying and hardly able to speak. I didn't understand what she was trying to tell me. I didn't know who or where she was. "Just tell me where you are," I asked her. "I don't know. Here is a river, plenty of water," she said. Maybe she was trying to run away but the line got cut. I waited to hear from her again. Days and months passed, and I only have the memory of those rattling words.

When I wake up I have a message from him, saying that he was in Syria to help with a rescue operation.

"Thank God you're back safely. How are you?" I asked.

"I met with some smugglers and we came up with an alternative plan because the usual route is being bombed by fighter jets. We don't know whose they are. Unfortunately one of our girls died with the smuggler in his car because of the bombing."

"That's awful. It must have been a missed target."

I heard Abdullah's phone ringing.

"I think there's someone on the other line."

"I'll call you back."

"Okay."

When Abdullah called me back, he said, "That was someone who helped me save a kidnapped girl who didn't know we were trying to rescue her."

"How?"

"Her uncle heard about the place she was being held. One of the survivors had been in the same building with her. We sent someone to stake out the area. He sat there for hours selling tamarind juice, hoping to see her – but her story isn't like all the others."

"How so?"

"She didn't want to come back with us. She wanted to stay with Abu Sulayman."

"So how did you get to her, then?"

"Her cousin, who had been with her, escaped and then told her uncle that Madlin – that's her name – was totally disoriented, and that she was in love with a Daeshi. Madlin refused to leave him, but she was given a sleeping pill and rescued while she was asleep. Now she's threatening to kill herself if we don't let her go back to her 'husband.' He went to visit his family in Saudi Arabia during the Muslim holiday and he left Madlin 'on loan' with his friend. Abu Sulayman had given Madlin his phone number in case she needed anything. She called him and they agreed that she could go and live with him. He told her to wait at the end of the street where he would send her a driver to take her to Saudi Arabia. But the man who was monitoring Madlin for her uncle picked her up instead. He drove her to Iraq. The whole time she thought she was going to be with Abu Sulayman in Saudi Arabia."

"That's really strange. I wonder what made her get so attached to that Daeshi? Was he different from the others?"

"I heard he used to play with the kids in the building, that he was nice to them. Madlin is a child herself – she's only fourteen years old. When he went to Saudi Arabia and left Madlin with his friend, he would call to check in on her, reminding his friend to treat her well."

"Maybe it's Stockholm syndrome? I don't understand how it happens but maybe that's what happened to Madlin. Or maybe it's because of Daesh's cruelty in general, that any act of decency seems to be somehow virtuous by comparison."

"Whatever the case, she's feeling better now. She doesn't mention Abu Sulayman anymore. She even says that she feels as if she's awoken from a strange dream."

"It must be very odd for a Daeshi to ask a friend to treat someone kindly, huh?"

"Really. But would you like to hear something else that happened to another woman we just welcomed back? Would you be able to handle Maha's frightful story?"

"All the stories you've told me so far are frightening, as far as I'm concerned."

"Well, when I went with Maha to the Office of Kidnapped Affairs to document her case, she wasn't able to speak because of what had happened to her. It was that horrifying."

"What happened to her?"

"First they sold her eldest daughter and then, after tying her up and beating her, they killed her three sons right before her eyes."

"Why did they do that?"

"Because she'd tried to escape and she had to be punished."

I didn't know what to ask Abdullah next, so I remained silent. After a few moments, he said: Maha was pregnant when they took her and her husband and four kids – two daughters and two sons – from Kocho. Her husband was thrown into a ditch and killed along with the other men. Then they took Maha and her kids to a medical institute in Sawlakh, east of Sinjar, where they separated the older women from everyone else. Sixty-seven grandmothers were set aside – some of the grand-children refused to be separated from their grandmothers. The men from Daesh didn't force them, and instead dug a big ditch: they threw all those grandmothers and grandchildren into the ditch and covered them with dirt. They buried them alive. The younger women and the children, about six hundred in all, were sold in bulk to a Syrian merchant named Abu Ali for a hundred and fifty dollars each. Abu Ali sold them off individually. A man named Khalid bought Maha. He took her and her kids to the Manbij region outside of Aleppo. Khalid was the director of the Aisha hospital. Just imagine a Daeshi as a hospital director!

"I felt sick all the time," Maha said. "I didn't know if it was from my pregnancy or from the situation I was in. After two months in captivity, I gave birth to my fifth child. I didn't name him. I said I'd name him later, but I didn't have the desire to do anything – he didn't have a name or any milk."

Maha had to mash rice to feed her baby. There wasn't any-thing else to eat or drink. One day, when the baby was three months old, Khalid came home with another man. Khalid told Maha's eldest daughter, who was fourteen years old, that she had to go with this man because he'd bought her. Maha cried and begged, and the kids surrounded their sister so that she wouldn't go with him, but it didn't make any difference. Khalid forced her aside and ordered her to go. "A deal is a deal," he said. Maha dreaded the day that Khalid would sell her second daughter, who was twelve years old. She decided to run away with her children as soon as possible. The first time Khalid went to go to the hospital, she and her kids left the house. Her daughter helped her carry the three babies, who were three months, eighteen months, and three years old. They crossed a few streets and then they stopped outside a store. Maha asked the shopkeeper for directions to the bus station. But her Arabic was poor so the owner was suspicious. He reported her to Daesh. Khalid was well known in the area, and it didn't take long for him to leave work and retrieve them. He took them back to his house; he tied Maha and her daughter to the bed and beat them with all his strength. The three babies were in horrific pain because of the poison he had given them. They died, just like that, in front of their mother and sister. Khalid buried them in the garden because "they're infidels, and they don't deserve to be buried in graves," as he put it. Maha fainted next to her children's little graveyard. She fell down and stayed right there, refusing to leave them.

A few days and nights passed. Maha remained frozen in place, motionless – a statue next to the graveyard. This attracted the attention of the woman next door, who used to avoid Maha. But when she learned about what had happened, she began visiting Maha all the time, offering her help. One day, she offered to help them escape. Maha didn't respond. She had turned to stone, and no words would come out of her mouth. But her daughter responded. The neighbor brought her cell phone so that Maha's daughter could call her uncle. I received a message from him on WhatsApp. When Khalid left for the hospital, Maha and her daughter waved goodbye to the neighbor and left. My plan for their escape started in the park by the hospital and ended with them walking to Zakho. When I received Maha, she asked me, "Are you Abdullah?" She knew my voice because I had been with her on the phone every step of the way. She hugged me, crying, and said, "What good is it that I survived? I wish I had died there with them. I wish they had buried me in that garden."

I wanted to reply to Abdullah, but the words wouldn't come out of my mouth either.

ONE STEP CLOSER, TWO STEPS, THREE

She whose song
has no beginning
nor end –
She whose voice faded
into stars and moons –
Where is she?
Where is she?

"I have some good news. The mother returned finally."

"The mother whose child got across the border first?" I asked.

"Yes. It was so moving to receive her."

"Thank God she made it back safely. I'd love to be able to speak with her."

"I'll let you know as soon as I can."

Abdullah met the mother near the temple in Lalish. She was visiting the temple to renew her baptism. Abdullah held her baby so that she could finish the ritual. When she was done, she took her baby back, thanked Abdullah, and said, "I feel uncomfortable leaving my child with someone else, even if it's only for a few minutes. I imagine he'll disappear from right under my nose, and even if I run after him I won't be able to catch up with him."

"Is the second baptism a new ritual?" I asked.

"Yes, our spiritual leader called for it in order to purify tortured souls, those who were persecuted and forced to give up their religion. It's a ritual for returning to oneself."

Abdullah sent me a recording of the mother's story.

I imagine their steps, one step closer, two steps, three ...
    Their families are waiting for those steps to be heard, closer, closer still ...

I got a glass of water, closed the door behind me, and listened:

I ran ... I ran after my friend who was carrying my son but she crossed the border without me. There were deafening explosions coming from all around us, but I kept my eyes trained on the two of them. They crossed over quickly with the others. A group of armed men prevented me from crossing. The area was filled with men I didn't know. We didn't know them, or what they wanted from us – anybody could kill me or rape me or sell me. I heard the sirens of successive ambulances ... I was afraid to die and leave my son without a mother or father. I wanted to reach my brother and ask him to take care of my son in case something happened to me. But time was running out, time slipped past me and I couldn't catch up with it. There wasn't even time to cry, but tears streamed down my face silently. A policeman stopped me and the others who were trying to cross the border. They detained us until further notice. I told the policemen: "I don't want anything from you. It's not my intention to stay in your country. I just want to cross and return to my country. I just want to cross. Nothing else. Nothing, please ..."

They said they would release us when the investigation was finished; they said that these were just routine security measures. In fact, that prison was much nicer than the Daesh house. At least I wasn't raped there. I don't know why I was released or how I crossed that distance ... I can't remember everything ... But as soon as I was across the border I saw all of them – they were all there waiting for me. We cried ... We cried so much ... We sat on the floor to cry as much as we wanted. My friend who had carried my son for me was also there. I hugged her with indescribable gratitude. I couldn't believe that I had woken up from this nightmare ... But I've found some comfort here in the Lalish shrine's baptismal water. It's so relaxing to be barefoot here, exactly the opposite of being barefoot around Daesh. It was so disgusting to be enslaved by those people with their filthy beards. At least our sheikhs here have clean beards and they don't hurt anyone. Soon I'll be going to Germany with the other women because they have specialists there to treat us. But after the treatment, I'll come back here. This land is sacred and we can't leave it, no matter what happens. This isn't my first time visiting Lalish. Every time I come here, I untie a cloth knot that had been tied by another pilgrim and I retie it as I make a wish. This time my wish is so precious, the most precious in my life. I only say it in my heart. If I tell anyone else, it won't come true.

Then I listened to the recordings of five others who had visited the temple to renew their baptism after returning from captivity:

What should I tell you? I don't know where to start. I was working in a hair salon, and my husband was a teacher in the Kocho secondary school. We were earning a decent living. I loved my husband even before we got married. Once, when I visited him at school because he had forgotten to take his lunch with him, I saw how much the students loved him. In the hallway they fought over who would get to carry his lunch for him. Who could have imagined that beasts would overrun the school and turn it into the site of a massacre? I saw them from the second floor of the school, when they killed my husband along with the other men. Our newborn baby was resting on my shoulder. My husband was a skilled musician and I used to sing when he played the lute. We always had friends over who would stay up late and sing with us. My husband didn't want to leave his lute at home that day, that cursed day when Daesh attacked us. When they separated me from my husband, I yelled, "Why are you doing this? You have no right!" They replied, "We'll take you all up to the mountain. You're just being separated temporarily." They laughed at us. They tricked us so that we wouldn't scream and cry. They only delayed our tears for a little while.

What can I say? My son is a lot like his father. One day I'll tell him about his father and what he was like. I'll give him the lute when he grows up. But I've changed a lot as well – I even forgot the songs ...

They emptied the region. Only the sheep remained there – sheep without their shepherds. Our animals were left alone, without any supervision. Nothing had ever hurt me before, but with Daesh everything in my body was hurting. From childhood we are accustomed to opening our eyes and seeing the sun and nature. Even though we weren't guilty of any crime, they imprisoned us inside four walls; our souls were tortured inside our bodies from the humiliation and cruelty. It was so hard to breathe. If not for my kids, I would have killed myself – I endured everything for them. My favorite thing to do there was mashing the rice into soup: I mashed it with all of my strength because I badly needed to crush something. I wanted to curse at him but I was afraid that he would harm my kids. That would be the worst punishment. One time I dared to defy him by asking, "If you had a sister, would you let someone treat her the way you're treating me?" He didn't hit me then, which was unusual because he would hit me whether he had a reason or not. He calmly told me that he was doing the right thing, implementing *shari'a* law. Even when he raped me, he justified it by saying it was a kind of "worship." He ordered me to pray with him before raping me.

But something else that was strange happened to me in the Daesh house: my relationship to my husband's second wife changed dramatically. She was with me in the same building and we would meet when the Daesh men left to fight. Our shared pain made us unexpectedly close, so much so that I wouldn't escape without her. She courageously confronted a Daeshi when he tried to rape my eldest daughter, who was twelve. "Leave her alone," she shouted, "she's just a child, what do you want with her?" Her words had cost her so much, her words turned this man into a wild animal, and he beat her in a way that he'd never done before. She was in a lot of pain and I hugged her as she cried. Our friendship became deeper than I ever could've imagined, especially since I'd once considered her my enemy – after all, she took my husband from me and my kids. But she didn't take him forever, as Daesh did. We'd been married for ten years when I first noticed that he'd changed, that he didn't care about me and the kids the way he once did. He was out all the time, and even when he was home, he seemed absentminded, as if he wasn't with us. At first he justified being away all the time by saying how busy things were at work. He worked at a dairy that he owned with one of his friends. He complained that the cows were sick and that it was affecting his work. But deep down I sensed there was another problem that had nothing to do with the cows and their diseases. My feelings were correct. One day he came and confessed that he was going to marry another woman. It wasn't shocking to me because I'd been expecting it, even if I had hoped that it wouldn't happen. I always foresee the things I'm afraid of. I don't know if it's intuition or the embodiment of my fears. I even anticipated Daesh's arrival – I felt that some evil was going to come, and I was scared before it even happened. We were waiting for the Daesh men to go away, for the chance to run away together – Neeran, her daughter, my three kids, and myself. All of a sudden, I couldn't understand what was happening exactly, but their phones all started ringing, and in a few moments the five men picked up their weapons and left in a hurry. We heard the revving of the car's engine and then absolute silence. All of us, all the women and their kids who were captives in that building, ran away. Without looking back, we separated ourselves into groups, and moved in different directions so that we wouldn't attract any suspicion. Our group – Neeran and I and our kids – walked for about two hours, hesitating to talk to anybody; you don't know how to tell your friend from your enemy. A man who was walking on the opposite side of the street with his two kids didn't seem evil to me, so I stopped him and asked if we could use his phone. He said okay. But I was disoriented and couldn't remember a single number, so I handed Neeran the phone. She called several different numbers but nobody was picking up. The man didn't lose his patience with us, he didn't mind us making all those calls. Finally her cousin answered. Neeran returned the phone to the kind man and asked him how to get to the bus station. The man pointed us in the right direction. He didn't give us a chance to thank him. He quickly continued on his way. We walked about another hour until we reached the station. We needed to call Neeran's cousin again so that he could tell us what to do next. He said he'd ask around and would have an answer by the time we called back. "You decide who we should ask to borrow their phone," Neeran said. "Your instinct is always right." I took a long time to decide. I was afraid to ask the wrong person. That would mean death for all of us. When I glanced at an old woman sitting on a big rock, I knew she was the right person to ask. She told us that she didn't have a cell phone, but she called over a young man who was standing nearby. This man, who was possibly her son or her grandson, I couldn't tell, gave her his phone. Neeran's cousin picked up and told her to find a driver who was carrying diapers with the number three on them. A long period of anxiety passed for us when we weren't able to find this man. It felt like a tunnel with no end. I'm not sure how much time passed: maybe an hour and a half, maybe more, maybe less – time was passing in an unusual way. Anyway, we finally found the man we were looking for. It took us three days to escape. With every step we took, the shadow of Daesh receded. Now that we arrived, their shadow is far away from us, but it hasn't disappeared. Their frightening faces come to my mind and appear in my chats with Neeran. We decided to live together, to raise our four kids. I never imagined this would happen. I had even once told my husband – who is also her husband after all – that he was crazy to suggest that we move in with his other wife and newborn daughter. He's still missing. If he ever returns, he won't believe that we're living together.

I found a way to be free: a small bottle of poison in the bathroom. I mixed some of the powder in a cup of water, and gave the rest to my friends who were captives with me. We all drank at the same moment, as if we were toasting our freedom. None of us died, but we all got sick. Death was a wish that didn't come true for us.

The men weren't with us that day, and we would have been able to escape if the door had been unlocked. The female guard locked it behind her when she went to sit in the front garden. We watched her through the window as she talked on the phone. We call it a "garden" even though it only had a few withered trees. The woman seemed European, she spoke formal Arabic with a heavy accent; she seemed to be extremely knowledgeable about the Daesh laws, which they called "*shari'a* law." She had special status among them. She acted as a leader, sometimes as a secretary. She would give them orders after receiving a phone call. One day, that woman disappeared. I don't know if she returned to her own country or if she died. Her absence didn't make a difference, though. The men still locked the door.

Before my captivity, I was engaged to a man from Zakho. I met him during the spring festival of Nawruz, when I took a trip with my parents there to visit my uncle and spend the holiday. My uncle took us out with his family for a picnic, where we joined the other families in the area who also went out to celebrate the Eid. My cousin introduced me to Isam. I caught him smiling at me when we were dancing in a group. It was April, the month when the red tulips bloom – our people hang bouquets of tulips on their doors in order to ward off evil. We don't milk our cattle on the holiday – on this occasion, the milk is for their own calves – because on the Eid everything should be complete, happy, and beautiful.

We unfolded a big blanket under the tree and sat on it for dinner, just as the other families did. Every family picked a tree to sit under. I watched Isam put the same types of food on his plate that I'd put on my own. We were eating and chatting and I learned so many things about him – his interest in science, his optimism about solar energy. He was serious, but he also had a sense of humor that I liked. I found myself thinking about him during the trip back home to Sinjar. Before long he called me up. He asked me for the recipe of the cake I'd made and brought to the picnic. He said he loved it and wanted to try to make it himself. We exchanged numbers – so I figured he would call me – but I didn't think it would be to ask about my recipes. But he called more than once, and was always sweet to me whenever he did. I was eager to meet him again. Isam moved quickly. He asked me to marry him before we'd even met a second time. As a matter of fact, I was very happy, it was the happiest time of my life. We were engaged and planned to get married after he graduated from university in less than a year.

Two months after our engagement, we heard about Daesh. Our neighbors were leaving their houses so we decided to leave for Zakho and stay in my uncle's house. Isam encouraged us to do the same because he'd also heard that Daesh was coming toward Kocho. On the way to Zakho, we found ourselves face to face with Daesh.

I ended up spending a year confronting those beasts along with the other young female captives from my village, in a house in the Deir al-Zor area in Syria. They raped us, beat us; they forced us to cook and clean and wash their clothes. During the day, they would take their weapons and go out. At night, they would come back and gather together to take drugs and recite religious verses. When they told us it was time for "Quran lessons," this also meant that they were also going to rape us, because they typically did that right after prayers. They would take naked pictures of us with their cell phones, and before starting each "Quran lesson," they'd exchange pictures of us with one another to see whether there was anyone who wanted to swap with them.

One day, three of them came home so exhausted – and one of them had been wounded in the leg – that they fell asleep without their "Quran lesson." As we watched them sink into a deep sleep, we all ran out, barefoot, so that we wouldn't make any noise. We were five girls walking alone at night. After about an hour of walking, we decided to knock on someone's door. We agreed that only one of us would knock, while the others hid, just to be safe. The youngest girl with us, who was eleven years old, offered to be the one who knocked. She told them, "I'm Iraqi and I escaped from Daesh." They invited her inside, and when she told them about the four of us still waiting outside, they let us in too. We stayed with that family for two days, meanwhile getting in touch with some Kurds and making a deal to smuggle us out for three thousand dollars each.

When I crossed the border into Iraq, my fiancé wasn't there with the rest of the people who'd come to greet me. I later learned that he'd joined the Peshmerga fighters. I was able to see him two weeks later when he came back from a mission in the mountains. He hugged me while I cried – he wanted me to tell him everything but he was upset when I told him how I'd tried to kill myself. "I went to fight those beasts for you, and you were about to kill yourself?" he asked. But then he seemed to understand when I told him more of the details of my suffering. "I would have probably done the same thing if I were you," he said.

Our wedding is going to be postponed until my mother gets back. She's still missing, and I don't want to get married without her there.

Oh, Muslim, come, there's a virgin in heaven. That's the beginning of the song that Abu Nasir sang for me every night before he raped me. He would take some drugs and get high to that song. One time I asked him what the song meant. "You're a Yazidi infidel. It's not your fault, you were born like that. When you die, you'll become a houri to entertain us, we Muslims," he replied. "Doesn't that mean you have to wait until we die to do what you're doing to us, since we are still alive?" I asked. "I bought you, making you my property. This marriage duty is part of the jihad," he said. Of course, I couldn't speak my mind freely with him. The main motivation for these Daesh men was sexual: they would kill anyone in order to rape women. In the end they would kill themselves to meet their houris in heaven.

Whenever Abu Nasir needed money, he would give me to someone temporarily, loaning me and then taking me back later. All I could think about was escaping but it took seventy days before I was able to steal the key from Abu Nasir.

I managed to escape but the terrible realization was that my family was all missing: my mother, my father, my three brothers, my sister-in-law, and her family. None of them ever came back. Now I live in a small tent with my aunt. In the next tent there is a girl who was my neighbor back in our village as well. We often meet, just like we used to do in the past, but not with that same sense of spontaneity. Five years ago, when my eldest brother left for Canada, I heard my mother say that he was in "exile," that she wished he would come home because "life in exile is difficult." The refugee camp is a kind of exile, too, then, and we are here as foreigners who can't be sure of anything. Everything seems temporary. In the past, we used to walk down the street, meet people, and feel good about seeing them. Now it's just the opposite. I don't want to see anyone. I want to be alone – but I'm not very comfortable when I'm alone either. Inside of me there's something enormous, something enormous but broken into pieces.

My wife Sawsan was expecting our baby any day, but Daesh paid no heed to that. They came with their black flags toward Wardia, our village that is next to Mount Sinjar. We saw a long caravan of people leaving the village, in cars, on donkeys, and on foot. But Sawsan wasn't able to walk that long distance and we didn't have a car or a donkey, so we stayed home. At night, looking through the window, Sawsan said, "Look, those are Daesh cars coming toward us." Then she turned toward me and asked me to take our four kids and leave. I didn't want to leave her there by herself. But she was so serious about it that she picked up a knife from the kitchen and threatened to cut her own belly if I didn't save our kids. Sawsan became hysterical and I tried to calm her down. I agreed to leave on the one condition that she hide in the sheep pen in the back of the house. She said okay. I supported her back with a pile of forage and gave her a bottle of water. I kissed her goodbye and left with our kids. We walked with the caravan toward the top of Mount Sinjar. My fear for Sawsan grew until it was taller than the mountain. From above, I saw Daesh fighters circling around the area where our house was. I couldn't take it anymore, so I went down the mountain but wasn't able to get all the way there. On the seventh day, I burst into tears. My friend who was with me suggested we both go to the house. "She must be dead by now," I told him. "We need a shovel to dig her grave and bury her."

It was after midnight and everything was quiet and desolate – it looked like Daesh wasn't there anymore. We went down the mountain and continued walking toward the house. The moment we arrived, my friend said, "Wait, I hear voices in the house." We waited for an hour and a half outside the house without going inside. Then I heard it. "I can hear someone humming," I said, "and it sounds like Sawsan."

I went closer to the sheep pen and saw Sawsan humming to the baby who was in her lap. She was sitting with her back facing me so she didn't see me. I whispered her name. She didn't turn around – she didn't move at all. "Sawsan, it's me, Murad," I said a little louder, but she still didn't respond. I went closer and walked around in front of her. I saw there was still some water in her bottle. I kneeled down and kissed her. I kissed the hand of the baby who was four days old and who had come into the world like a miracle. I carried Sawsan on my back and my friend carried the baby. "You'll get tired," Sawsan said. "Let me get tired. It's one tiny atom of your exhaustion," I replied.

We had to walk a little more than a mile to reach the others at the top of the mountain. Our four kids gathered around their baby brother. One of our neighbors donated his donkey to Sawsan so she could ride it on our way north with the other families. Now we're staying in Zakho temporarily and the baby is walking. He's seventeen months old.

NARJIS, NARJIS

I tried to imagine that birth, without a doctor or a nurse or a bed or any support from anyone; I tried to imagine how she'd suffered alone through that unbearable pain as she pushed the baby out of her body so that they both could be liberated.

I sent Abdullah a picture of two candles I'd lit for the sake of the two families he said that he was worried about. After five days, he replied, "Thanks for the candles. The two families arrived, and one of them is staying at my house."

"Are they relatives of yours?" I asked.

"Do you remember my niece Marwa?"

"She was the first person you rescued, wasn't she?"

"Yes. Her mother and her brothers made it here. Her two sisters and my brother, her father, are still missing. Please, please light more candles."

"How are the ones who made it back?"

"My sister-in-law Mona is unwell. I'll tell you about it some other time. Let's just say she needs to see a female doctor. As for her two sons, they're no longer the boys I once knew. They're a distorted version; their morals aren't those that my brother had brought them up with. They've been raised by Daesh, especially the older one. Just imagine, I have to tie his feet down when he goes to sleep. Otherwise, he'll try to beat my son when we all go to bed. He treats everyone like an enemy."

"Oh my God. He needs a psychiatrist."

"He was trained for violence day and night in the Daesh camp. I tried to win him over, I tried to bribe him – I offered to buy him a soccer ball or a new toy, but he said he'd rather have a gun. That's Farhad, the same boy who called me when he escaped with his mother and his brother and another family, saying that they didn't have any money to make it all the way back."

"So what did he think about running away after all that brainwashing?"

"One time, in the camp, the trainer ordered the two brothers, Farhad and Sarhad, to fight each other. He told Farhad: In the jihad, there's neither father nor mother, neither brother nor friend. There's only God. Now you are Farhad the mujahid. Suppose that Sarhad is an infidel, suppose he's your enemy, and you have to kill him – now, hit him as hard as you can. Farhad, who was fifteen years old, hit Sarhad, who was one year younger than him. He hit him so hard that he broke his front teeth. Sarhad fell to the ground, crying. The trainer grabbed a stick and broke it on Sarhad's body, telling him, *If you cry over your little teeth, how are you going to slaughter the unbelievers tomorrow?*

"Sarhad was moaning in pain. Farhad didn't care about his brother's teeth, and yet he was still upset that the trainer hit Sarhad – and he was moved by his mother's tears when she saw them and learned what had happened. They were usually allowed to leave for a day or two once a month, to visit their mother who had been taken as a sex slave by a man from Chechnya. He already had two Syrian wives when he bought Mona and her two boys from a Syrian merchant for four hundred dollars. That was twice the price the merchant had paid when he bought them from 'the market.' They separated Mona and the boys from the three daughters who were sold at an auction in Mosul. Mona had to work as a servant for the other two wives, and she was a sabya for the Chechen man. As time passed, a friendship grew between Mona and the older wife. She complained to Mona about her husband, saying that she couldn't stand him anymore. One day Mona and the wife came up with a secret plan to escape together.

"The day Sarhad came home with broken teeth, Mona told Farhad that she was going to run away with her friend and that he and his brother must join them. Mona expected Farhad to refuse but he seemed excited about the plan. When Daesh took my brother's family to Talafar, they called me and I told them to wrap my telephone number and the number of my son Mehdi in nylon so that they wouldn't get ruined by water. *Stash the piece of paper in your clothes*, I told them. At that time I was with my family and hundreds of families on the mountain. I went crazy because I didn't know what to do. I couldn't even tell my mother and my family about them. We were eating and I pretended everything was fine, but after I took my first bite, I left them and threw the food away. You understand how hard it was to swallow it."

"Yes, I know," I said, imagining how the world would shake with every bite.

"Farhad called me this time," Abdullah continued, "and informed me that they had run away when Daesh went to prayer. They didn't have much money, not enough to buy food or make another call, so I asked them to tell me where they were. Farhad said they were near a train station with some airplane debris in front of it. I told them to return to the same place the next morning – when everyone was at prayer – and that in the meantime I'd figure out where they were, and that there would be a car waiting for them, whose driver would be holding a bag.

"Things went according to plan, but when they arrived in Aleppo, they were stopped by an inspection patrol. When they found that they didn't have identity cards, they were detained, held in a building that used to be the Manbij post office. Farhad was able to make a quick call to tell me what had happened. I immediately headed out in their direction. On the way, I got in touch with the smugglers who work with me. One of them rushed over there on his motorcycle. It was time for evening prayer, so all the guards went to the mosque. Life completely stops during prayer because, as they say, the earth stops turning until prayer is over. This works to our advantage. In those few minutes that Daesh was away, the smuggler found the two families. As soon as he told them he'd been sent by me, Farhad clung to him and didn't want to leave his side. Perhaps he was scared. I was on my way to meet them. The smuggler called me and said they were safe. Of course, I was jumping for joy. But they ran into another problem when they reached the border. The Turkish police prevented them from crossing. The police started beating them with cables. The driver who took them back to Manbij left them in the street because Daesh fighters were attacking the area. Farhad called me again, from a shop-keeper's telephone.

"Once again I left my food on the table and went out. I spoke with the shopkeeper on the phone: *If you want to do a big favor, you can help us save this family. If you want money, you can have whatever you want.* The shopkeeper asked what he could do to help. *Lock them inside the store, and leave them there until I can send a driver for them,* I replied. *I can send the driver with as much money as you want in order to compensate you for closing your store.* The shopkeeper replied: *I'll do it for the sake of God. I don't want any money.*

"They survived thanks to that Muslim man who was nothing like the Daesh Muslims. But they still weren't safe yet, the problem still wasn't over. The new driver, who took them to a village near the Turkish border, called me, and said, *The son of the Syrian woman wants to return to his Chechen father. He's threatening to tell on us. What should I do?*

"*Give him a sleeping pill unless his mother decides otherwise*, I said."

Abdullah had an appointment with some French journalists so he had to go. But he called me an hour later, and said, "My guests were very nice. I asked them, *What would you like to drink?* They said, *We'll love trying everything.* So I brought them all the drinks that I had. Then I understood that they meant 'anything' and not 'everything.' So I told them we drink special coffee made from pistachio. They said they'd love to try it."

"I've never heard of that kind of coffee. Is it different from Arabic or Turkish coffee?" I asked.

"It's our own coffee. We extract it from a small green tree on the mountain. It takes longer to make and its liquid is thicker."

"My students tried Arabic coffee. They thought it tasted like mud."

"Our coffee is even thicker mud."

We laughed, and then he suddenly whispered, "Glory be to God, glory be to God."

"What is it?"

"There's a plant here sprouting out of the wood. Just like that, without any soil," he replied.

"Where?"

"Out in the open land."

"Take a picture of it for me. But what are you doing out there in the open land?"

"I'm walking to the market – here's the picture."

"It looks like a mushroom. I don't remember seeing that kind of a plant in Kurdistan. I remember the white and yellow daffodils that used to fill the streets."

"We used to give bouquets of *narjis* – daffodils – as gifts. People have no time for it nowadays. By the way, they've started using that flower a lot in alternative medicine, as an herb that calms the nerves."

"How many daffodils would we need to soothe our nerves?" I asked.

"I'd say that all of the daffodils in Kurdistan wouldn't be enough."

"*Narjis, Narjis* was the only Kurdish song we knew in Baghdad. It was so popular that we used to repeat the lyrics without knowing what they meant."

"So you've visited Kurdistan?"

"Yes, of course. Several times. Maybe I'll visit sometime to taste the pistachio coffee."

"I'll just leave the door open for you," he said.

I searched online for a picture of *narjis* to remember those days when I went on trips to the north. Once, I visited the Sheikh Metti Monastery on top of the mountain – by the time you make it to the top you're totally out of breath. But there you're rewarded by drinking the cave's fresh water, spending days in a world away from the rest of the world, where people become closer to one another, as if they have known each other since ancient times, sharing everything: food, beds, games, and prayers with the nuns. In the morning, there was always the smell of burnt milk ...

Once, I went to the north with my friends for fun. Another time I went to drink Erbil yogurt, and once to compete in Iraq's national chess championship. Fermseek of Sulaymaniyah was the best player among us, and the final round was between her and me. Our game lasted three hours. In the end she won, so I shook her hand. I stood up, and turned around to see a friend of mine standing behind me, who'd been watching the game. Right away she tried to lift my spirits by saying, "You were Black, that's why you lost. White has the advantage." In that moment, those words didn't mean anything to me. I wasn't aware of what it meant to have White's privilege – that white always plays first, that it was easier to lose as Black than as White, that if you're Black, losing is justified, if not expected. The first time I became aware of this issue was when I filled out my immigration form in America. I found a question about a person's color – black or white, among other ethnic identities. I wasn't sure which box I belonged to, so I chose "other." One of my relatives who lives in Detroit told me, "my neighbors are all black but they're not bad." Did he assume that I thought they were bad? But I liked that he also added, "Just like us, they love to break the law." The first black girl I met was in my sociolinguistics class at Wayne State University. When she learned that I was a poet, she offered to take me with her on a trip to one of the Michigan lakes where there were going to be poetry readings and jazz music. It was there that I read my poem "America," which was my newest poem at the time – that was my first reading in my new country. The modest audience received me by beating on drums, which really surprised me. I took a picture of the lake, where lilies floated on the water like Ophelia.

I noticed that people in America don't need censors like those in the Arab world: they watch themselves, limiting their speech within the boundaries of what's acceptable. In the Arab world, censorship follows speech. In America, censorship precedes speech.

People here have such beautiful dreams. To annoy Americans with our nightmares simply means inviting them into our underworld. America is still a young country, so it isn't always easy for them to understand us – we are the older ones.

I've heard from my relatives that Americans care more about their dogs than about other people. Maybe because human love is incomplete. As Iraqis, we don't have the habit of caring for dogs. Perhaps dogs are what we really need, to know the meaning of unconditional love. A dog doesn't care where you're from, it doesn't care about your race or religion or color. All the dog wants from you is to throw something toward the horizon, like a worry you finally brought out of your chest, so that it can run after that thing and grip it tightly between its teeth, panting and excited, as if the whole world has just been caught between its jaws.

In Iraq, we don't have the concept of "black" the way it is in America. The letter N doesn't mean "Negro" for us, but still it's a symbol of the enslavement of minorities and of genocide.

And in order to survive, we pretend that we are dead.

The last time I went to northern Iraq before leaving the country, I was with my family, escaping from the intense bombing of Baghdad in 1991 during Operation Desert Storm.

We were in the war room – that's what my mother called the little room under the stairs, its windows sealed with tape so it wouldn't shatter, its door frame also covered with tape so that no chemical could get through, and its shelves stocked with bread and canned food. Our room was shaking so intensely that we were surprised the ceiling didn't come crashing down on our heads. When the bombing quieted down, we headed to our ancestral town of Telkaif, north of Mosul – the birthplace of my parents. They moved to Baghdad after getting married, so my father could work in the capital. We arrived at my aunt's house. She reassured us, as soon as we got there, that the fighter jets wouldn't come to the village because "it's too far removed from any danger in the world." I remember how red her face was from being near the clay oven all day, where she baked for guests who filled the house. She refused to leave for Sweden with her eldest son, to join her other son there. "Sweden is too cold, my son, too cold," she said, "just leave me here – otherwise, who will remain in the house? Shall we just leave it empty? They say anybody can come and take an empty, forsaken house."

My mother was born in that house. My aunt had inherited it from her father, my grandfather, because she and her family were the only ones who stayed behind in the village. Everyone in the area knew that house because it was much bigger than the neighboring houses, and it had a circular shape. In its center there was a large, open patio, surrounded by rooms on all sides, and there was also an adjoining field with separate shelters for the animals – one for the cows, one for the chickens, and one for the donkey. They told me that the donkey knew the way home, in case I tried to ride it and got lost. My cousin wanted to teach me how to milk the cow but I didn't like doing it. My aunt would make yogurt from that milk – and no one could forget that taste. Now, twenty-three years later, the banner of the Islamic State was hoisted above the gate of Telkaif, and the cross was lowered from the church. My aunt and her family walked out silently, leaving the house as it was – with its clay oven, its stables, its many rooms untouched – overlooking the hill. I contacted them from Detroit to check in. My cousin responded immediately. There was so much eagerness in her voice, as if she were waiting for a call. "Where are you?" I asked her. "In Zakho now," she answered, "but tomorrow God only knows. We all left as soon as we heard that Daesh had arrived. We didn't take anything with us, not even the great golden halo over the head of the Virgin Mary. It was night, and the children were all asleep. Badri's friend in Zakho told him, *Those beasts buy and sell women,* so Badri hung up the phone and told us, *Get in the car right away. Leave everything, there's no time.*"

I asked her about Badriya, her sister who lived in Mosul. She replied, "Badriya also fled. First she left Mosul and came to us in Telkaif, but Daesh followed us here, so we moved north, and then farther and farther north. We don't know how far north we'll wind up. What can I tell you about Mosul? They canceled school, gave students CDs to teach them about violence and crime. The children were confused, women saw with nothing but frightened eyes, masked fighters roamed the streets, giving strange orders over loudspeakers: *Everyone must go and sign the repentance cards, otherwise they'll face capital punishment.* Cigarettes forbidden, birth control forbidden, music forbidden."

What hell it is to be a citizen in Mosul, I thought.

But now, this particular bit of information I'm reading

about the *narjis* gives me hope: one of this flower's secrets is that even though it shrinks away when strong rains fall, as soon as the sun shines it blooms back again. *Jinda*, as they say in Kurdish, meaning "coming back to life again." Maybe Kurdistan is a daffodil that has only wilted temporarily, only temporarily.

THE INFIDELS

I didn't hear from Abdullah for quite a long time. That worried me. He'd told me that he was busy trying to rescue his two captive nieces. "My daughter is going to be so happy to see them," he'd said. "They've been friends since childhood."

After that long absence, he wrote, "I'm very sad right now. Daesh caught the two girls and imprisoned them."

I called him immediately. His voice was strained like never before.

"I feel the same as I did on August third, when they were first captured."

"I'm so sorry to hear this news," I replied.

"When the opportunity finally arose for the two girls to escape, the only thing they didn't have was the Daesh outfit, a black dress and a burqa. I located them, and told them to wait at the Farouq Hospital in two hours, where someone would give them a bucket that is normally used to hold yogurt – inside they would find the necessary clothes. She rolled a black cloth around herself and went to the appointment, where she received the clothes successfully. The men had gone off to fight, and it was the perfect opportunity for the girls to run away. They wore the "shari'a-appropriate" clothes and returned to the hospital. I managed to make a deal with an ambulance driver to move them quickly from where they were in Aleppo to the Mansoura area between Raqqa and Tabqa. The two girls arrived at a safe house, and I was supposed to pick them up the next day and take them to my house. I didn't say anything to my family because I wanted to surprise my daughters. But someone from Daesh ambushed us. One of our smugglers had been waiting for some other captive girls, who were being monitored by Daesh. When those girls reached the smuggler, Daesh caught all of them. Daesh took the cell phone from them, and sent me a message after finding my messages on the phone: *The girls are safe now. Where should we take them next?* I gave them the location of my nieces, hoping that the other girls would join my two nieces as well. That's how Daesh found them. It was my fault. I've paid for it in tears and anxiety during the past few sleepless days ..."

"Who would have known the message was from Daesh? It's unimaginable."

"Daesh is very skilled with technology – they use the most up-to-date means to infiltrate their enemies. In fact, they keep gaining new members who are able to access meaningful information and use it to their advantage."

"I agree with you, especially when we consider their Hollywood style of self-promotion."

"So our work is not without its challenges. Our rescue operations have failed on more than one occasion. Several times I've lost money from my own pocket. This week, after the arrest of my nieces and their smuggler, in a moment of despair, I paid a very large sum of money to a Daesh worker as a bribe, so he would negotiate their release. But this Daeshi later claimed that he had tried but was unable to do anything. He didn't return the money I'd paid him. After a week of terrifying silence, someone else called me and said he was living in the house next door to the headquarters where my nieces were being kept. He sent me their picture and offered to assist in smuggling them out of Raqqa. He asked for six thousand dollars. I agreed again, as I would pay everything I had to bring the girls home – and to bring some happiness to my two daughters. He told me that he would drive the girls toward the Euphrates along with his wife so as not to arouse suspicions, since families in Raqqa usually go to that area for picnics. But after I had transferred the money to him, I realized that our messages were being automatically erased from the phone screen. I asked him about this. He told me that he had a program to delete them for security reasons. He wrote to me under the name 'Saleh Shami,' warning me, *If you receive a message from me with a different name, don't reply. That would mean that they've caught me.* Anyway, he promised to take the girls away from Raqqa at 3:30 p.m. I sent my crew to the agreed place at the agreed time. The girls weren't there. We waited three hours without any sign of them. I couldn't fall sleep until dawn and he didn't respond to me until six in the morning. In his message, he apologized for not responding earlier, signing off with the name 'Ahmed Shami.' I didn't know if 'Saleh' got caught or if he had deceived me. *Who are you?* I asked him. *I've got the texts between you and Saleh. We're going to cut off his head,* he replied. And things ended just like that. You see, there's no law to protect us, and we'll just have to take matters into our own hands. A lot of people in Raqqa work with Daesh, directly or indirectly. They're all cousins. What can we do? We have to deal with them in order to save our people."

"It's so much pressure."

"But I'll never lose hope. Anyway, my nephew's wife ran away from Daesh successfully thanks to a friend of mine. I'll call you tomorrow to tell you her story and the story of Idrees, who helped her. How does that sound?"

"I'll be waiting."

The next morning I was walking to the park in my neighborhood in Michigan. The birds were remarkably loud, and they attracted Abdullah's attention when he called me. "Michigan must be fantastic with all those birds," he said.

"It is, especially in the fall. But it's so cold in the winter. I hope you can visit us one day."

"Why not? And I want to visit Canada. I have friends there."

"Michigan is close to Canada."

"If only we had birds' wings. Do you know the *qabaj* bird?" he asked.

"No."

"It's one of the most beloved birds in Kurdistan. It's said that hunters forget where they are when they hear its beautiful song, so they follow the sound of the bird wherever it goes, leaving everything behind. You writers are a lot like the *qabaj* hunters."

"I love this metaphor. I'll quote it."

"And now, my friend, are you ready to hear today's story?"

"Of course."

Abdullah began: When my nephew Falah got engaged to Nidal, all the members of our tribe were astounded because she was seven years older than him – he was only eighteen years old. But he looked very happy on his wedding day. It was obvious that he was in love. The wedding was great and it was held jointly between them and another couple. We all danced the *dabka* in a large circle around the two couples. Nidal's father was so moved because she was his only daughter. Her mother had died during her delivery.

The couple was blessed with a girl and a boy. They named the girl Farah (Joy) because on the day of her birth her father got a job as a policeman on the border between Iraq and Syria. They named the boy Faraj (Relief) because his father escaped from the grip of Daesh just days before he was born. Falah was on a mission in the Ramadi Province when Daesh attacked the region and captured many police officers. Falah managed to escape with some of his colleagues, hiding in the valley for three days without any water or food. When they saw a wandering ewe, they milked her and drank the milk.

Six months later Daesh invaded the area, so the rest of the family ran away with the villagers who went to the mountain. Like the others who ended up with Daesh, the family was trapped at the edge of the mountain; then they were captured and separated from one another by sex and age. Nidal didn't see her husband after that day. They took her to Talafar, selling her with the other women. The man who bought her had to stop in the middle of the road and take her to the hospital because she'd fainted. The doctor said her condition was critical, and he recommended that she be transferred to the Mosul hospital. The man took her there. Waiting in the lobby, Nidal saw Idrees, who is my friend; he's from the same area as Nidal. He was sitting right there in front of her. As I told you, in our area everybody knows everybody. They only exchanged a few looks, however, too afraid to speak to each other. Idrees was able to write his phone number on a scrap of paper, and slip it in her hand when the Daeshi went over to the receptionist to sign a form. Nidal hid the paper inside her veil, which she'd been forced to wear by the man who bought her.

After several medical tests, Nidal was diagnosed with severe dehydration. They treated her with a lot of fluids and medications. She felt better, but as soon as she and her man arrived in Raqqa, she fainted again. This time the man took her back to the Qaqa market and exchanged her for another woman. "This woman is sick," he said, "and she's no good to me." Daesh are allowed to return and exchange women like we would something at the shopping mall.

She was returned, and they assigned her to the kitchen to cook for Daesh and the other captives, since she was too skinny to be sold again right away. Food for the captives was very scarce, but she was sometimes able to steal some of the Daesh food and give it to her two children and the other captives. Five months after she was put up for sale again, Nidal and her kids were purchased by a man she described as "ugly and old." Once they arrived at his house, he called his wife and asked her to "raise this infidel family." He would beat her first, then have sex with her. Even after she got pregnant, he wouldn't stop beating her whenever she refused to have sex, complained, or said she was sick. Even on the day she gave birth she wasn't free from his commands. He took the newborn girl away from her and didn't allow Nidal to breastfeed her or even hold her. "She shouldn't drink from the milk of the infidels, only from the milk of the Islamic State so that she'll become strong and, in the future, a martyr on the path of God," he said.

Nidal became even weaker and skinnier, and she was no longer able to do much of anything. This Daeshi also returned her to the Qaqa market, along with Farah and Faraj. A Syrian man bought them for two hundred and fifty dollars and took them to his home in Raqqa. He lived with his mother and his four brothers. His mother welcomed them, saying, "You are

fortunate to be given shelter even though you are infidels."
Nidal recalled: *His mother was very harsh with us. Whenever
Faraj cried she would get so annoyed that she would ask her
sons to get rid of the child. They would beat him and I could
hardly protect him from them. One time when Faraj wouldn't
stop crying one of her sons picked him up and said, "I'll toss
him off the balcony." I ran after him but not fast enough. He
actually threw him off the balcony. I raced down; Faraj was
moaning. He was not dead but wounded: his hand was broken.
He wasn't even two years old. They refused to take him to the
doctor but the neighbors who saw me crying and begging for
help offered to take him. The doctor treated his wounds and
put his hand in a cast. The mother kept watching me all the
time. Even when the neighbors went to the doctor with me, she
sent a guard to look after me. I was fed up with life. I called
upon the Lord to help us survive or die – anything other than
living with that woman. One day I heard the loud sound of an
airplane, and I wished that it would bomb the house, even if
we all died. My wish came true a few seconds later. The plane
bombed the building next door, and the house caved in on us.
I lost consciousness for two hours, and didn't wake up until
I heard the voice of my daughter Farah. She was holding my
face, screaming, "Mama! Mama!" The three of us got up from
under the rubble, emerging from the big holes, all covered in
blood. People from the neighborhood rushed over to us. That
cruel woman was screaming and howling. Four of her children
had died right in front of her. They were crushed under heavy
blocks of rubble. One son, supposedly my husband, wasn't
in the house at that time. When he returned to find what had
happened, his mother said, "You have to either kill or sell
these infidels. I can't look at them anymore."*

Their next owner took them to the doctor to have their wounds treated. The doctor discovered that Nidal had an advanced stage of diabetes. "Maybe it was caused by the shock of the bombing," he declared.

The necessary insulin treatment wasn't available in Raqqa, but it was in Mosul. The man sold them to someone in Mosul for the sake of the insulin. Finally, it was there that Nidal was able to use the piece of paper that Idrees had given her. She called Idrees and he gave her my number because he knew that she was my nephew's wife. In those days Idrees was a recent survivor, having just made it back to our town. Nidal wasn't able to write down my entire number because the Daeshi had seen her. He grabbed the phone away from her and reprimanded her. Days passed – he went off to fight in the Battle of Kirkuk, and he came back completely exhausted. He fell into a deep enough sleep that she was able to steal his phone, call Idrees, and write down my complete number. Just then, the man woke up and leapt at her, seizing the phone and my number. Nidal trembled in fear. She expected to be killed. "You're calling someone in order to escape, aren't you?" he said.

Nidal didn't reply. To her surprise the man dialed the number and said to me, "Nidal is here. I'm prepared to sell her to you for thirty thousand dollars."

"Well, give me a little time to get the money together, and I'll transfer it to you," I replied.

The man kept calling me every day even as I continued giving him excuses to stall for time, saying that I couldn't transfer the money yet because the banks were closed. A week later, Nidal called me and said in a hushed voice, "Listen to me" – then she raised her voice – "where are you, brother? I'm calling you from the phone of the *munasireen* group. I need to know when you're going to return."

"I'm in Ba'aj fighting the infidels," I said.

"When are you coming back?" she asked.

"Tomorrow. Just give me the address," I said.

"Al-Muhandiseen District in Mosul. There's a public park close to us, in front of Aladdin's Celebration Hall," she said.

"I'll meet you there tomorrow at 4 p.m. If I don't make it tomorrow, then the day after," I said.

The next day the smuggler told me that he'd waited for two hours but didn't find anyone in the park. The day after that, I received the good news that they'd made it to the park. Once they got into the car, the smuggler gave them new clothes and removed the cast from Faraj's hand so Daesh wouldn't be able to identify them. Faraj's body was covered in scars, but they couldn't be seen under his long-sleeved clothes.

They'd reached the Mosul Dam by the time her owner called me and said, "Nidal ran off."

I pretended to be surprised: "Tell me the truth. Something happened to them, right? An aircraft bombed them or something?"

"Do you mean to say that you didn't know? I'm sure you're behind their escape, you infidel," he said. He kept insulting me in text messages, so I blocked him ...

Abdullah got back to me after we'd been interrupted and had to hang up more than ten times. When he called me back, he continued: You must be wondering what Idrees was doing there at the Mosul hospital? He was undergoing medical treatment as a member of Daesh. But let me start from the beginning ... Idrees decided to get a ride with Daesh when they announced that they were going to take the Yazidis up to the mountain, into Kurdistan. Daesh had brought their cameras, telling everyone, "We're going to film you announcing your conversion to Islam so that you'll be safe. Otherwise you're going to have to clear this region for us, and then we'd take all of you to northern Kurdistan."

All of them chose to leave, without any hesitation. Just then, Idrees remembered that his grandmother was still in the house all by herself, and thought that it might be better for her to go with them. He got out of the giant vehicle that could fit forty people and ran back to his house, which was fifty yards away from the car. He came back with his grandmother. Daesh, who had given him permission to go and was waiting for them, indicated that the grandmother should ride in the car for women, and that Idrees should wait for the second convoy. The men in the first cars had just been thrown into those deep ditches and shot dead – Idrees heard the sound of gunshots and wondered what was happening. "There are clashes underway. That's why you're hearing those sounds," Daesh answered.

It was time for the second convoy to leave, and Idrees got in. But at that moment he realized the danger they were facing. There were a dozen others with him, including his twenty-year-old son and his older brother. They were all thrown down together. The Daeshi pointed his gun at them as he told them to line up next to each other. Idrees stood in front of his son to protect him, while his older brother crumpled in front to protect Idrees. Someone was groaning but Idrees didn't think he'd been injured, and the Daeshi fired a second time, then a third, and Idrees was hit in his feet. Another Daeshi shouted from the back: "Did you make sure they're all dead?" The Daeshi turned back toward them. None of the wounded were moaning. They left, and there was complete silence. Idrees remained frozen in place. He was badly hurt, not only because of the gunshots in his feet but also because he was sandwiched between two dead bodies, one was his son and the other was his brother.

Idrees stayed like that, pinned in place, wanting to cry, but no tears came out of his eyes – he didn't want to leave behind his two loved ones who had passed away without him. He remained there for many hours, hoping to die so that his pain would come to an end. Idrees was neither dead nor alive; he was completely detached from everything, yet at the same time connected to the two bodies next to him. What would he tell his wife if he saw her again? How would he possibly tell her about the death of their son? She used to check in on him all the time, counting the days until he would come back from studying law at the University of Sulaymaniyah to spend summer vacation with them. But where was his wife now? And where was the rest of his family? Where were they going to be taken? What would happen to them? Idrees finally decided to pull himself out of the ditch. He tore his *dishdasha* and wrapped the wounds on his feet with it. After several attempts to climb out, Idrees finally made it. It was a very dark night, the worst night of his life. He walked with difficulty toward the village of Serdar, but he didn't make it very far – he was so exhausted that he lay down beside some okra leaves. He could see fields of wheat and barley in front of him – the farmers must have abandoned them without gathering the harvest. Idrees lowered his head and spotted nine men running after some other men and shooting at them. He saw them fall to the ground one by one. There was a fire, and a plane hovering above the burning field. He wished that the plane would land and carry him high above the fire, but it flew away and disappeared.

Limping in a hurry to get away from the fire, Idrees noticed a few houses scattered on the edge of a plateau in the village of Biskay. He knocked on the first door he saw, asking the man who opened the door for some water. The man went inside and came back with a large blanket; he wrapped Idrees up in the blanket and threw him down into the valley, saying, "You couldn't find anyone else's house?" Idrees had bruises all over his body, but he was awake, in a strange state. As he lay there after falling, he saw two men walking toward him. Idrees was worried they would kill him, so he decided not to ask them for anything. The two men stopped in front of him. After a few moments of silence, one of them extended his hand to Idrees and asked, "Do you need anything?" Idrees replied hesitantly, "Water." The man said, "Come with us, our home is nearby." When they arrived, the men didn't invite Idrees to enter their house, but directed him to the chicken coop behind the house. It was a three-foot by six-foot space. They brought him water and milk, and told him that he would have to leave before sunrise. "That's fine," he said, "but may I also use the phone?" He couldn't remember any of his friends' numbers except for one that was very easy to remember: the number of a shepherd he used to spend a lot of time herding with – Idrees would wake up early to take his sheep out to the plains, but the day of the Daesh attack he went out with the sheep to accompany his friend, puzzled about why there were so many lights piercing the darkness that night. They were the headlights of the cars carrying people who were fleeing their homes as Daesh attacked like locusts on the fields. Those who didn't own cars rode on donkeys; others walked. Idrees was among those who'd stayed in their homes.

It was a good thing that his friend picked up the phone during that critical moment. "I'm bleeding, and I don't have much time," Idrees said, "can I stay at your place for a little while?" His friend apologized, saying it was too far; it would take an hour and a half by car. Before he hung up, Idrees heard a voice on the other end: "Is that Idrees? Give me the phone, I want to speak with him." Idrees knew who it was at once. It was Musab, one of his best friends from the same part of Kocho. "Where are you, Idrees? No, I won't wait until sunrise. I'm coming to get you right now," Musab said. Musab arrived a few hours later and helped Idrees into his jeep. On the way back, Musab asked a lot of questions – the first one was more of a protest: "The chicken coop? Shame on them. They don't know how spoiled you are. But your feet are swollen, Idrees. You need medical attention."

Musab decided to take Idrees to the hospital right away. But on the way he changed his mind because, when he called his brother, he learned that Daesh controlled the area. His brother advised him to go see a medical assistant that he knew instead. The medical assistant successfully stopped the bleeding of Idrees's feet – applying some hydrogen peroxide and wrapping them tightly in gauze – and then gave him some antibiotics. Idrees was supposed to follow up with him in two weeks when he ran out of pills. During the two weeks he spent at Musab's house, Idrees noticed the wound on his right foot had become redder. And it was still hurting him. The medical assistant advised him to go see a specialist at the Mosul hospital. "But Mosul is under Daesh's control," said Musab. The medical assistant was silent for a few moments, and then said, "If you want to trust in God, and go to Mosul, I know a judge over there. He used to live in Kocho but moved to Mosul to work at the court. He stayed there despite Daesh being in control. I heard he's one of those judges who stamp the identity cards of the Islamic State. Would you like me to refer you to him so that he'll help you get into the hospital?" Musab and Idrees exchanged looks and then Musab said, "We'll trust in God, as you said, and go to Mosul."

On the outskirts of Mosul they were stopped at a checkpoint. Musab showed them his identity card. Idrees didn't have one so he remained silent. Musab said, "This man is a shepherd, he works for me. I brought him to see his sheep." The inspector didn't say anything – he just shrugged them along. Musab drove Idrees straight to see the judge.

The judge received them without getting up from his chair. "What's your full name?" he asked Idrees. When Idrees pronounced his name, the judge said, "Get out, all of you. Only Idrees stays." Musab and the others who'd been waiting to meet with the judge went away. Idrees became afraid that the judge had suddenly become agitated when he heard Idrees's full name. But to Idrees's surprise, the judge started sobbing like a baby. Idrees couldn't see him because of the curtain between them. Finally, the judge asked, "Are you really the son of Bashar Sillo? From Kocho?" Idrees confirmed this. "I know your father very well," the judge said, "tell me, what do you need?"

Idrees replied, "I need an entry card to the hospital." The judge handed him a piece of paper, saying, "Listen, whenever anyone talks to you at the hospital, let this be your response: *God willing, on the road to martyrdom.*"

Idrees entered the hospital, and as soon as the receptionist looked at his card, he called for someone to come and accompany Idrees to the waiting room. It was there that Idrees saw

Nidal and managed to give her his phone number. The hospital was full of wounded Daeshis. Idrees lay on the bed next to theirs. Idrees wanted to look at them, to try to understand what kind of human beings they were – and why they were doing this to him and to his people. But at the same time he didn't like looking at them. He didn't want to know them. The doctor came in minutes later, and before examining him, he said, "God bless you. You have been wounded for the sake of the Islamic State." Idrees replied, "God willing, you are on the road to martyrdom." As he was leaving, someone with a long beard entered the room. He seemed well known to all the other Daeshis. Everyone paid attention to that man, perking up at the sight of him. This important man walked around the beds greeting the wounded and giving them each a hundred-dollar bill. But Idrees refused to take money from this man who'd contributed to the death of his son and his brother – and God only knows what had happened to the rest of his family. "I'm going to donate it to my brothers who are fighting now," Idrees told the bearded man. "God bless you for taking this stand," the man said. He called in the doctor and said, "This man should be given the finest treatment." The doctors and nurses in that unit gave Idrees priority, coming down to check on him every hour. In addition, they gave him extra medication and medical supplies, enough to last him two months. In the end, the nurse released him from the hospital by saying, "You're a crown above our heads."

Idrees returned to Musab's house. The wounds on his feet had started to heal. But the wound in his heart had not. None of his family members came back. He called one of his relatives and asked, "Who from my family has made it back? Has anyone returned?" Idrees threw the phone away, and picked up the pistol near Musab, in order to kill himself. But Musab swiftly jumped on top of him and wrestled the pistol away from him. "What if your family comes back and doesn't find you here? Who ever said they're not coming back tomorrow?" Musab said, adding, "I'll take you to Dohuk, brother. There's an Office of Kidnapped Affairs there. Maybe they can help." Idrees collapsed into Musab's arms, crying, and in a tremulous voice said, "Who's going to receive me? How can I go on with my life? I have no one, no one."

Musab called me, and mentioned that he was bringing Idrees to our city. He asked me to gather together as many acquaintances and friends as I could to greet Idrees so that he wouldn't feel lonely. When Idrees arrived, there were more than a hundred people waiting for him. When he saw us, he sat down on the floor, weeping.

SINJAR: THE BEAUTIFUL SIDE

At the edge of a mass grave, Abdullah stood there crying. He had finally found his brother:

He was sleeping
on his side
just as he always does
except that his bones came into view,
you can even count them.

Surrounded by friends
as usual
except they're dead.

Completely calm
not worried about his wounds.
He never did as a child
except he'll never grow up.

Close to one other
like two conjoined trees
on which they would rest their backs
except now they have no words

Over the mass grave
the sun slips through the clouds
like every time
except today it makes death brighter.

With a trembling hand, Abdullah pulled his phone out of his pocket to take the call. He was still staring at his brother's corpse as he spoke with the latest captive who was trying to escape with her children. Later, Abdullah would leave his brother's funeral to go and receive that family. "I must respond to his death by saving even more people from the hands of the killers," he said.

If we go back to the village, will we be in the mood to plant?
What would we plant on the land filled with bones and
skulls?
What would grow?
How much blood would flow in the veins of the trees?

November 13, 2015 was a bittersweet day for the people of Sinjar. It was the day Sinjar was liberated from the grip of Daesh, but it was also the day the mass graves were revealed. They contained hundreds of bodies of men, of women who were unfit for sex, and of grandchildren who refused to be separated from them. They were among the hundreds of thousands of Yazidis who'd left their homes and marched in a long caravan, kicking up the dust in the road behind them, because the barbarians came, their black flags on the carts of the caliphate. Those carts that would escort the sabaya to the fortresses of the mujahideen emirs. Along the roadside, new signs read: "God willing, the Islamic State Endures" and "No Entry."

Sinjar, or Shengal, which means "the beautiful side" in Kurdish, looked very much like a wasteland. Scattered along its ancient roads were bones and skulls, clothes and shoes, utensils and car parts, amid the ruins of the burned-out houses and farms, looted shops, and gutted temples and churches. An old clay goblet is all that remains of the Virgin Mary Church in Sinjar. My friend Kamil Zomaya pulled it out of the rubble, saying, "This holy cup alone survived all the destruction. Daesh destroyed one part and the air strikes destroyed the other."

I asked Kamil about his family. He said he had just buried his mother in the village of Teleskuf.

"I'm very sorry for your loss. Are there people still in Teleskuf?"

"No, not a single living person. Only the dead. They don't allow anyone to enter except the dead and those who've come to bury the dead. I spent my childhood in that village. I can still hear the sounds of chickens and donkeys. Today you'll hear nothing but the wind. You would be scared to walk down those dreary alleyways."

"I wanted to visit Telkaif, the village of my ancestors' graves."

"Telkaif is also empty. People fled there as well. The whole village is in the hands of Daesh."

The grass grew up on the graves until it became taller than the dead ...

"The beautiful side" is now "the land of mass graves." Some journalists named it "the liberated city" – after a Kurdish official stood atop the hill, placing a microphone on a bag of sand, and declared the liberation of Sinjar. At the same time, he warned people that there might still be land mines there. "And beware, some Daesh fighters are still hiding in the city," he added.

The people of Sinjar are now dead in those hastily dug trenches, prisoners of Daesh, displaced in the camps, or survivors who are wounded in their souls and in their bodies.

"Who liberated Sinjar?" I asked Abdullah.

Abdullah replied: I'm not sure, but one of the people who helped liberate the city is Sulayman, a twelve-year-old boy who was a zealous fighter even though he wasn't technically allowed to fight because of how young he was. When Daesh attacked Sinjar, Sulayman was at home with his mother and seven siblings – three sisters and four brothers. His father was out of town for work. The Daeshis in those days would come and go, telling people, "Convert to Islam and you'll be safe." About three hundred people from the village gathered together to discuss this call to convert to Islam. Sulayman's mother suggested that they tell Daesh they'd already become Muslims, lying to avoid harm. Sulayman didn't like the idea that his family would agree to convert to Islam just to avoid the evil of Daesh. Sulayman was a distinguished student at his school. He liked to talk about everything and asked lots of questions. His mother's response that they were only converting to Islam temporarily didn't make any sense to him. She didn't want to speak about the matter anymore because she was busy talking with their father on the phone. His father was concerned and wanted to come back. She told him to stay where he was until things cleared up, and said that she was going to do the same thing as everyone else in the village: hand over all her money, gold, and guns in exchange for peace. And she didn't notice that Sulayman left the house without telling them. It was nine o'clock at night, and he had to walk twenty miles to reach the mountain. The sun rose and set, and Sulayman kept on walking, with only two liters of water. Finally, amid the beanstalks on a farm, Sulayman lay down behind a harvesting machine and slept. When the sun came up again, he opened his eyes and saw a caravan of people from afar. He got up, ran until he caught up with them, and walked alongside them. He arrived with them that night at the mountain. In the meantime, Sulayman's mother was beating her breast and crying. She called her husband and said, "Daesh kidnapped Sulayman or killed him. He left the house and hasn't returned. They must have taken him off the street."

The next day Daesh came and took the villagers in their big cars. Sulayman's mother asked them, "Where's my son Sulayman? Bring him back so that he can come with us." But no one paid any attention to what she said.

Sulayman's father didn't know what to do. His wife had stopped responding to his calls. His anxiety increased when he heard that Daesh had captured the people in the area and had taken their cell phones. He was by the Beesh Khabur bridge over the Tigris, helping some of the people who were fleeing. He had hoped to find his family among them. After going back and forth several times, he saw his son Sulayman with the others. He rushed over to his son, asked him about the rest of the family, but Sulayman had been wondering about them as well.

News spread that Daesh had killed all the men and taken the women as sex slaves. Sulayman was so upset by the news that he couldn't calm down. He left at noon, telling his father that he was going to meet some friends. He came back in the evening with a gun. Sulayman announced to his father that he had volunteered to fight Daesh with a group of Yazidis. "You're young, my son, and this gun is too heavy," his father said. Sulayman explained that he was going to liberate Sinjar. The liberation of Sinjar was random in the beginning – people were going out to fight without any military guidance. But a year later the volunteers joined the Peshmerga army. Sulayman was younger than the legal age to join the army, so they refused to take him with them to the battlefield. Sulayman begged them, saying that he was even ready for suicide operations against Daesh, but they refused his request. In response, Sulayman killed himself. Ever since then, Sulayman's father always carries that gun with him, and goes out as if he were headed off to war.

For the people of Sinjar, you can't call a place home unless you can plant on it. They don't count age by the years, but by the seasons of harvest. They know locations not by address, but by traces of life. Places are known by their proximity to the mountain, to the valley, to the hill, or to the cattle farm. Their trees have roots that extend back to the time of the Sumerians, who invented the wheel so the earth could go around.

"I wonder, Abdullah, now that Sinjar is liberated, do you ever think about returning to your home?" I asked.

Abdullah answered: Nobody from Sinjar has gone home. They wrote the letter Y on our homes and on our stores, and built a barrier like the Berlin Wall – N for the Christians, and Y for the Yazidis. S for the Sunnis, and Sh for the Shi'ites. At least they allowed the Christians to leave, even if they had to go empty-handed. They didn't extend such "privileges" to the Yazidis.

Overall, it seems like the jihadis follow a certain pattern of invasion. First they refer to their prey with a particular letter, an X or a Y. Then they offer the victim peace in exchange for money and weapons, but later break the agreement, taking the money and the weapons without offering peace. Then they justify their actions by saying it's God's law. This is what their caliph says: *O my brothers, what don't you understand? If we prevail against the enemy infidels, it's only natural that everything should become our property. The people should be our spoils, our captives. What else would we do with the female captives if not distribute them to the jihadis? In order to create this system, we need to open a market where we can sell the sabaya and their children. Each head has a price. If the share of each jihadi is five people, for example, and if he didn't need all of them but needed some money, what would he do? It's simple. He would sell some of them at auction. The law of God says that those who weren't present at the invasion have no rights to the spoils. Isn't that just?*

One of my friends on Facebook commented on this caliph: *Brother, you're killing me, displacing me, and raping my wife and my sister because you want to implement the law of your God. Please tell me where this God of yours is so that I can sue him for damages.*

Have you ever checked out the Daesh websites? They attract a lot of attention, despite how strange they are – but perhaps it's because of their strangeness. Lately someone has been egging on the new jihadis, reminding them that there are seventy-two houris waiting for them in paradise. He told them: *Hurry, hurry up and register your names, the houris are waiting for you in paradise, where you can eat and drink with the Prophet.* And someone answered him: *I am for jihad. I am for jihad.* Then they kissed each other, exchanging congratulations.

It seems to me that the promise of paradise is the golden idea Daesh uses to win over young guys – using both modern and older means of communication and propaganda, as well as to linking the past of the caliphate with the promised paradise. And their chanting, along with the verses, raises the adrenaline level of the fighters so much that they forget everything but the black flag fluttering in front of them.

"They fight in the name of God and the houris," according to Nadia Murad, the young woman who lost seven people in those mass graves – her mother and her six brothers. "In those exposed mass graves, the bones of my mother and my brothers and the rest of the dead are left to be swept away by the rain or eaten by animals. People ask me what I need – I need to bury my mother with dignity."

Nadia said: "The daily routine for Daesh is taking drugs, reciting religious songs, going to fight, and then coming home and raping women. I ran away several times but I didn't get away. They punished me by continuously gang-raping me until I lost consciousness. I barely survived because a kind family from Mosul helped me. They were Sunni Muslims like Daesh – but they were not like Daesh at all. They took care of me, helped me return home. They even apologized, saying, *We're sorry for not feeding you well enough.*"

Nadia – as sad and transparent as a teardrop – said to her therapist, "I don't want to talk about what happened to me here in this closed room. I want to talk to the whole world." And she did. Nadia spoke with members of the UN Security Council, making them cry – her words spread from country to country: "They glued our pictures to the walls of the court building so that members of Daesh could pick from the pictures the ones they wanted to buy or sell. Like any Middle Eastern girl, I came from a conservative society. No man is allowed to touch us before marriage, but Daesh simply exploits us for sex and fun. They beat us, they force us to pray, and they force us to serve them food in porno outfits. While I was raped by more than a dozen men of various nationalities, I thought about my mother – how much I just wanted to hug her. I missed my siblings and their children. My mother raised us on her own after my father died in 2003. I was in the high school literature section. I loved my village. I had a simple and happy life with my extended family, which consisted of twenty-six people. When I was held in captivity for three months, I wished for the world to end. The problem isn't that the world is going to end, but that it continues without any change."

Nadia has changed a lot since being with Daesh. It can be seen quite clearly in the before and after pictures. It's as if she'd aged a decade in a single year: "Every part of my body has been transformed in their hands," she said.

Psychotherapist Dr. Nagham Nozad Hassan told me that she visited Nadia in the Khanki Camp after Nadia had a nervous breakdown. "I was struck by how smart, attentive, and brave Nadia is. By chance, I had received a proposal to transfer a number of Daesh victims to Germany, so I added Nadia's name to the list."

"Dr. Nagham, you meet with survivors on an ongoing basis. What's the most difficult situation you've ever confronted?" I asked.

"The psychological turmoil of survivors who got pregnant when they were raped – their conflict of feelings between motherhood and the desire to get rid of Daesh embryos."

"You're also a specialist in gynecology, right?"

"Yes, but I closed my clinic after Daesh attacked. I decided to work with the United Nations instead – this disaster is far more important than any normal work."

"You already won the International Women of Courage Award from the US State Department – how did you earn that?"

"I would visit the camps on a regular basis to do what I could for the survivors in helping them return to normal life."

"Is it possible for them to return to normal life?"

"Not really. Still, we're trying to find a way to give them some sense of dignity, at least."

I followed up about Nadia when I spoke with her brother Sa'eed. He was one of those who was shot, but didn't die.

"What do you remember most about Nadia before Daesh?"

"I remember the holidays. We used to wake up early to meet our friends. It was our custom to visit those who'd lost loved ones to offer them our condolences. I'm the eleventh child in the family, and Nadia is number twelve, the last one. She was still really close with our mother. She liked school – and she was doing so well there. We had a large farm and a big house, which was always filled with guests who came over for our parties, to eat and drink with us. They were the same people who killed us and captured our women later."

"How many of the twelve are still missing?"

"There were eight of us who disappeared, but my brother Khalid and I got away after they shot and injured us. You've already spoken with Khalid, he mentioned."

"Oh, I didn't realize that Khalid, Nazik's father, was your brother, Nadia's brother. Please send him my regards," I said.

"I was in the group before him. The person who shot me

used to be my neighbor. He said, *Come down from there, you dogs.* He shot me six times in my left side, my neck, my back, and my foot. I heard the engines of their cars rev when they left. My friend Dilshad asked, *Is anyone still alive?* Four of us were still alive, but one person couldn't move because his injuries were so serious. The other three of us crawled out of the mass grave. I was bleeding from my entire left side. I kept walking and falling, then trying to get up again. Near an electric generator I stopped and packed my wounds with dirt to slow the bleeding. There, I told Dilshad to leave me behind because his wounds weren't as serious as mine. I stayed there for six hours, just a hundred and fifty yards from the mass grave. I watched the others bury the dead. It was maybe eight o'clock in the evening. Some low-flying planes passed overhead. Then I walked about four miles, arriving at the village of al-Qabusiyyah at around midnight. My body was swollen when I knocked on someone's door. The people in that house welcomed me inside, and gave me some painkillers. It was a Muslim family – my feelings toward them were a mixture of gratitude and distrust. I stayed with them for six days, and then walked twenty miles east, toward Mount Sinjar. I was bleeding again, falling onto the ground, wavering between this life and the next. In the end, a group from the Patriotic Union of Kurdistan found me and handed me over to the Kurdish government. They took me in an ambulance to a hospital in Zakho. I stayed there for twenty-two days. Then they took me to an American hospital in Erbil, where I stayed for ten days. That was when Nadia called me and told me she'd escaped from Daesh. My three other sisters were still captives. As soon as I was discharged from the hospital, my stitches still clasping my wounds, I signed up to fight Daesh. When Sinjar was liberated,

I was among the first to enter the city. While I was there I saw my mother in the mass grave. Now I have the opportunity to go abroad, but I won't leave this country before I have contributed to the total liberation of my people."

Sa'eed stood up and pointed to his village on a large map hanging on the wall of his tent.

"Did you really see her? Your mother?"

"I saw her identity card in the midst of bones and other remains."

THE SPRING

Twenty years after leaving Iraq on a one-way ticket, I returned to my country today, on May 27, 2016, not so much to visit the living as to visit the dead.

We, the people of Baghdad, used to refer to the north as a "resort" – it was our only tourist destination when travel was forbidden during the 1980s on account of the Iran-Iraq War. But this isn't tourism today. We came to visit the mass graves, perhaps to bury our feelings, too, and to get rid of their weight upon our souls – or perhaps because they needed us, they needed us so much and yet we didn't go! Or because we're alive, and we can, quite simply, visit the dead.

But the one survivor I most wanted to see was Abdullah.

"Peace be upon you," he said formally, smiling. I had expected him to be dressed in white Yazidi clothes, not a modern outfit. We had agreed to visit the temple of Lalish together because, as the sacred Yazidi texts say, "the earth wasn't satisfied with its condition until Lalish was revealed; only then did the plants grow, and did the earth become beautiful."

I asked him if he was busy that day with a rescue operation. He said that he was.

"May I come with you?" I asked.

"Are you sure you want to do that? You have a US passport. It would be risky."

"I'd like to witness the process firsthand."

"Okay, but memorize my phone number, in case you need to be rescued."

I laughed and said, "Okay, I'm ready."

"You actually believed me? Not today. Besides, I wouldn't take you with me to Syria – let's go to Lalish instead."

We drove almost forty miles, along winding roads to the east of Dohuk, toward Sheikhan. The temple looked small from the outside but as soon as we entered, it opened up to infinity. We walked in barefoot like the others did, because "there should be no barrier between the foot of the entrant and the temple's floor." Our feet touched stones that were over 4,000 years old; another world opened up right before our eyes, in the depths of the mountain, somewhere between myth and reality. The narrow pass, surrounded by three mountains, gradually opened wider, revealing all that it had, like the generosity of its people, but sometimes it also closed in on itself, like the Yazidi religion.

As we entered a courtyard, there was a man sitting with a little sparrow in his hand. Abdullah introduced him as Luqman Sulayman, "public relations guy for the temple. If you have a question, he's the best person to ask."

"Nice to meet you. Yes, I have a question. Who's this bird in your hand?"

"This bird fell from a nest. I put him back but he fell a second time. After the third time it happened, I took him home with me. Now I've become very accustomed to his companionship so I brought him here with me."

Abdullah asked Luqman to let me enter the sacred places that are typically forbidden to non-Yazidis. "She came all the way from America to visit Lalish," Abdullah said. I didn't understand Luqman's reply because he spoke in Kurdish. It seemed to me that he wasn't going to allow it, but he did kindly invite us to have tea.

I would soon enter into those places without knowing they were "forbidden." Abdullah didn't seem to notice, or maybe he forgot, or simply didn't follow the instructions. Whatever the case I was pleased to be given those additional secrets without even realizing it.

"Careful, you can't walk on the thresholds. You have to cross over them," Abdullah reminded me.

I didn't count the number of entrances; it seemed to me that each of them told a story of the age. The entrances were so low that even a short person like me had to hunch down to get inside. To the right of one of those entrances was the snake of Noah, which is considered sacred by the Yazidis because it's said to have saved mankind when it curled itself up and plugged the hole that had been punctured when Noah's ark collided with a rock during the flood.

You pass from one cave into another, as if history is sleeping and you are inside its eyelid. I noticed colorful pieces of cloth tied around columns in one of the caves. Abdullah nodded at me encouragingly as I untied one, making a wish as I retied it: wishes are supposed to come true when another visitor comes to untie it. I glanced at Abdullah and saw that he was doing the same thing as me.

Next Abdullah picked up an untied medium-sized cloth, then stepped back a ways, closed his eyes, and threw the piece toward a stone outcropping at the top of the cave where there were already many other pieces of cloth. "You have to do the same thing, for good luck," he told me. I imitated his motions but didn't succeed. My piece of cloth didn't land in the desired place – I'm the worst basketball player in the world – but he insisted that I try again. "You have to close your eyes, and imagine the target," he reminded me. I succeeded on the third attempt. He probably didn't notice that I'd opened my eyes a little bit.

We went deeper into the cave until it became completely dark. Abdullah turned on the flashlight on his phone and raised it up to illuminate the place. I was very grateful for this person who sanctified light. We reemerged from the darkness and went into another cave. On either side there were very old stone pots. Pointing toward them, Abdullah explained that the olive oil in those pots was used to ignite wicks, and that Yazidis celebrate the new year in Lalish by lighting 365 lanterns, to usher in the new year with light. Their New Year's Day falls on the first Wednesday of April. They call it Red Wednesday because people put red flowers on their doors. "Did those rituals change after Daesh invaded?" I asked Abdullah. "We still light the lanterns because they give us a sense of hope. But we canceled all the musical festivities until people can return to their homes," he replied.

We went down several steps, descending into a deep cave there; there was a spring called Zamzam, whose waters branched outside the cave. I drank from it just as Abdullah did. He said it was considered the freshest water in the world. He didn't tell me then that the sacred water was for Yazidis only; it had something to do with their baptisms. Just a few steps away was the tomb of Sheikh Edi.

"By the way, what did Mr. Luqman tell you?"

"He said everything is permitted except drinking the spring water."

"But I drank some!"

"I know."

When we came out of the spring, some men and women were sweeping the floor. "There are always volunteers here cleaning the temple," he said as I glanced at a broom on the wall. I was embarrassed to leave like that, so I volunteered to sweep a little bit.

Every so often I would stop to contemplate those symbols carved onto the walls of Lalish. I was in awe of the fact that they were so similar to the Sumerian symbols that I'm so obsessed with – these symbols were the first form of communication in history. I don't know what they mean; like any great words, we can't know exactly what they mean. Poetry came first, through metaphors and images that referred to their meanings and their shadows. Among those symbols is the eight-pointed star, which represents the goddess Ishtar (Inanna), the circle inside the circle, the ornamental square, the sun disk, the palm tree, the sparkling pot with water flowing from both sides, and also the wings drawn not only on birds but on humans as well. The special bird for the Yazidis is the peacock, because, according to the Yazidis, "it's the head of the seven angels." They say the peacock was sent by God to alight on Lalish and brush its seven colors over the valley.

Pilgrims rest on big stones that have been eroded into the shape of seats without armrests, just like in ancient Mesopotamia. Abdullah sat down on one of those rocky seats in order to answer a new call for help.

"There's a family on the road. I'm following their progress step by step," he said.

Leaving Lalish, I looked out the car window at a tree, its branches so colorful with all the pieces of cloth tied around it as wishes. How many of those wishes will come true? And how many of the missing will return?

I met Abdullah the next day at a house he rented in Dohuk. We sat on the floor with his family. Abdullah was surrounded by kids, not only his own, but also the sons and daughters of his missing siblings, as well as other kids whose fathers were missing – he was taking care of all of them. They sat around him the way elementary students gather around their teacher.

There was a big lunch spread out in front of us, like those that tribal leaders would offer their guests. Abdullah put his phone down and said, "The family I told you about has made it to safety."

"That's wonderful. Now I have some of my appetite back," I replied.

After lunch, I was excited to taste the pistachio coffee. I love coffee, in general, but the taste of this special brew was so exceptional that it made traveling those thousands of miles worth it. Abdullah gave me three large packets of that coffee, saying, "Take this back to America with you."

"One is enough," I said, but he insisted, like a prophet who knows an eternal truth. His wife Sari wanted to send me off with milk to add to the coffee, but I assured her, "There's milk in America."

After we finished our coffee, we hurried to Qadia Camp to meet some of the people whose stories I'd already heard – but now we would meet them face to face. Abdullah unexpectedly slammed on the brakes several times during the trip, to make way for a flock of sheep. When we reached the entrance to the camp, he told me, "It's better if you take off your seat belt." I realized just then that he wasn't wearing his.

"Why?"

"So that you look like a real Iraqi. That way they won't

question you or demand to see a visitor's permit, the way they do with most foreigners."

We headed down a dirt road leading to the camp; tents lined the road, their residents who'd survived seemed as if they were living an ordinary life – a life like any other. They were cooking outdoors, drinking tea, bathing in the outdoor baths. Some children were playing with a ball, as if they were at a picnic, just like when we go camping with our families in America. But their eyes weren't like the eyes of others. The way they look at you: they turn back at you, as if waiting to hear some news from you, or perhaps they're wondering how you're going to just leave them so soon? Their eyes glitter with the evidence of everything that they've seen.

Behind the crammed tents, there is the United Nations sign and a girl jumping rope. Her feet floating upward give one a sense of emancipation. These children add movement to otherwise desolate places – but who could know the damage that had been done to their tender souls?

I was ready to listen to terrifying stories as soon as I arrived and started to meet the people there. I was stunned by their willingness to offer me help rather than ask for it. Their generosity has remained, despite the change in their circumstances. I didn't speak with a single person in the camp who didn't insist that I have dinner with them, or at least have something to drink. "You can't do that. We have to offer you something." They confront you with those words even as you're thinking about what you can do for them.

These people, whose stories I'd heard over the phone, are now right here in front of me, in the flesh. I simply greet them, without knowing what to do next. Shush, I think to myself, don't ask any more questions, don't reopen their wounds

– just say a few simple words, like the ones you would use with ordinary people in everyday situations.

On the way back from the camp, I took a few pictures, but I was stopped by a policeman, who said, "Photography is forbidden." I didn't know how to respond, but Abdullah hurried to speak with him in Kurdish. They talked for a long time, and the tone changed from officious to friendly. The policeman bid me farewell, but I didn't understand a word he'd said. In the car I told Abdullah, "You never told me photography was forbidden here." He replied, "Come on, there is a law, but that doesn't mean we have to obey it. As long as we aren't hurting anyone. By the way, that policeman is a relative of mine. He forgot all about photography and started asking me about some of the missing people." Just then, I saw some girls sitting on a red barrel, drawing on pieces of paper. "I want to get out there for a moment," I said. I took their picture and asked one of them, "What are you writing?" "Riddles," she said. When I showed Abdullah the picture, he said, "Nice. You had to take a picture of those girls."

Some of my old friends heard that I was back in the country. They hurried to put together a poetry reading. Poetry wasn't on my mind during this urgent time, but they said that I couldn't leave the country without reading some of my poems. It only took them three hours to actually organize the reading, including all the preparations and spreading the word on social media. That was the same amount of time it took for me to get from Dohuk to their place in Erbil. The road was very dangerous by car; every time the driver passed the cars in front of him by veering into oncoming traffic, leaving only a tiny distance as the drivers were forced to swerve suddenly – and every time I automatically threw my hands up to cover my face. I didn't expect too many people would show up for that last-minute reading, but I was wrong. Some of the audience included writers I'd known a long time ago, when I had just started writing poetry. How had they grown so old, with gray hair glittering on their heads? Maybe they were wondering the same about me, too. In any case, it seemed that poetry was still alive among my people. They wouldn't let me stop reading; they clung onto my words as if they were actually going to save them.

On the way back, I was startled by the sight of men sitting on the side of the road, counting piles of money and then putting the piles into garbage bags. I said hello to one of them, Emad Noury, a theater actor. He explained to me that it was payday. "The director brings our salaries in these bags every month," Emad said.

I remember the period of economic sanctions on Iraq, when the value of the Iraqi dinar fell so low that the currency had to be printed on such cheap paper that those stacked piles of dinars weren't worth as much as a dozen eggs. Still, the sight of cash carried in garbage bags was unexpected for me, coming from America. It was as if I hadn't experienced such things too during the first thirty years of my life.

Emad invited me to visit him at Amal Camp, so I went there. I thought I was going to see tents scattered along both sides of a mud road like in Qadia Camp, but this camp was actually a five-story building. We climbed the stairs to the second floor, to the room where Emad lived with his wife Hiam and their daughter and son.

A large 2016 calendar hung in the middle of the wall, with a sewing machine underneath. I asked Hiam, "I wonder what the 2017 calendar is going to be like?"

She was silent for a moment, then said, "Maybe next year will actually be as beautiful as this year's calendar wishes to be?"

She went into the shared kitchen, and came back a few minutes later with a tray of coffee and some candy we used to call "sour-sweet," which I remembered from my childhood in Baghdad – people would always offer it to their guests.

"Hiam, where are you from?"

"From Bakhdida, in Nineveh Province. Our home is there, two stories we built with our own hands, brick by brick."

Hiam showed me a picture of her house. Looking at it, she told me: "I was a sewing instructor. My friends and neighbors often stayed up late at our house, until well after midnight, chatting and listening to *tarab* music. When we heard about the arrival of Daesh in the region, Emad decided that we should leave everything and go, but I refused. I told him to take the kids and go. I was staying there, sure that he would return in a few hours. In fact, I was busy sewing clothes for my sister and her family because they'd just received their immigration papers to go to America. They were planning to leave in the next few days, and they needed new clothes – and I wasn't going to leave before I'd completed their clothes. It was 11 a.m. on August 6, 2014, when Emad and the kids left. Hours later, the sound of gunfire was so loud that I could no longer hear Emad's voice on the phone. In the evening, my neighbor knocked on my door and asked me if I wanted to leave with them – they had an extra seat in their car for me. I hesitated. What if Emad and the kids came back? My neighbor said, *Everyone is leaving and nobody's coming back. Come with us, Hiam. Don't stay here by yourself.*

"I went with them, and left everything behind except my house key. Emad had taken the photo albums and wedding tapes. There was nothing else of any value except for the house itself. I called my sister, and she said: *Don't worry about the clothes. The situation is terrible. We're going to the monastery near our brother. We don't know when we'll be able to leave the country.*

"I left with my neighbors – the road to Erbil was so crowded that it took us seven hours instead of one hour. We saw crowds of people running barefoot; some people rode on farm vehicles – not everyone has a car, you know. The sound of gunfire was even louder once we were on the road. That caused more confusion and delays at the checkpoints. The policemen in front of us told us to lie down on the ground. Daesh was behind us, waving their flags. Emad and the kids had made it to a public park in Erbil where they spent two days and nights. To reach them felt never-ending. I'm an optimist who's usually pretty easygoing, but what happened to us was completely unprecedented. We had lived through continuous war but we had never heard certain words like *sabaya*, *caliphate*, *fucking*.

"When I got to the park, it was so full of people there was nowhere to walk. I caught a glimpse of where Emad and the kids were, and I reached them by zigzagging between the families. They had sandwiches, which were donated by a family in town who handed out food to everyone in that park. We stayed there for a few days, and then we were taken to this camp. Emad is a theater actor, as you know, so he founded a theater group here in this camp. He started teaching and training the children here. They meet on the fifth floor for cultural and artistic activities."

"So there's a school here in the camp?" I asked.

"Yes, they go for three to four hours a day – and even do homework, despite everything."

"It's such a good thing to have classes in these extraordinary times."

"Our life is always extraordinary, you know. How do you find Iraq after all this time away?"

"Sour-sweet, as always."

I left Amal Camp for the shrine of Dair Mar Elia because I had an appointment with Claudia. She was introduced to me by a friend who volunteered at the Shlomo Organization for Documentation. At first, Claudia seemed withdrawn and reluctant to talk to me on the phone. But when we met I found her to be such a warm person, even aching with her kindness and deep pain. After the meeting, we cried and laughed together, and shared news like old friends.

Overnight the shrine of Dair Mar Elia had been turned into a camp that housed hundreds of displaced families from Mosul and the surrounding villages who didn't know how long they were going to stay there. Claudia's room was full of paintings she had recently made, "to release her feelings," as she says. In the middle of the room, her daughter Maryam was twirling around and around in her white dress, which looked too big for her, while singing softly in a mixture of Arabic and English. In another month, Maryam will be two years old. "Mimi memorizes what she hears on YouTube and sometimes combines unrelated lyrics," Claudia explained.

We went together to a café near the camp, staying late into the night. Little Mimi was very attentive, and every time she noticed someone leaving the café, she would say, "They just left." Claudia took some pictures with me, and said, "These are only for you. They're not for publication, except for a picture of this tattoo."

She shared her story with me: I was pregnant with Mimi when I heard about Daesh for the first time. I was shopping in the market, and I'd left my son Hawar with my neighbor to play with

her kids. But an hour later, she called me and said, "Come back, they say there's a gang named Daesh that is about to attack us."

It was around this time of year, about two years ago. On my way back from the market, I called my husband at work and said, "Get ready, we have to get out of Mosul. The situation doesn't look good."

I worried when my husband didn't come home from work that evening, and my concern grew with the escalation of gunshots nearby and the darkness surrounding our neighborhood. I called him several times but he didn't respond. I shared my fears with my neighbor. She said, "How could he respond to you while he was serving at the front? The world is upside down there. Of course he isn't going to respond."

But I kept trying to reach him, until morning when I fell asleep for a bit. When I woke up I saw that my husband's friend had written down his telephone number on a note that he stuck to our refrigerator. I called him. He said, "Our region has fallen to Daesh. Let me call our friends who were with him, and I'll call you back." I kept the phone in my hand until it rang. The friend said, "I don't know what to tell you … Daesh slaughtered him along with two other people he was with. One of our friends, who hid behind the water containers, saw them beheaded."

His words turned me to stone. The whole world became a stone that I wanted to throw away from my house. When my son saw me frozen in place like that, he asked what had happened. "Your father's dead," I told him. I was too shocked to consider his feelings. He sobbed in the corner.

Some neighbors had celebrated Daesh's arrival, even crying with joy, and throwing candy. The Daesh were smart. When they entered the city, they tore down the concrete barriers and checkpoints, which were annoying and upset many people. They provided water and electricity. But a month later they started imposing strange laws. For example, unmarried girls would have to wear white veils; widows, green; and married, black. They banned shaving and makeup. Modern clothes disappeared from the market. In the mosques they shouted for everyone who worked for the government to repent, and to swear on the Quran that they had forsworn any political party. On July 17, to be precise, they issued a law that Christians had to pay the *jizya*, but even that tax wouldn't necessarily save anyone. They marked the houses of Christians with the letter N, announcing that those houses had become the property of the Islamic State. My Muslim neighbors apologized, saying, "You were here in these houses before us. It's not right to do this to you."

I didn't know where to go. My parents hadn't spoken to me since 2003, when I got married against their will. I'm Christian and my husband is Muslim. His parents were angry at him for the same reason; he declared that he had become a Christian. My parents told me, "You're not our daughter anymore." His parents told him, "You're no longer our son." Our love was too strong to kill. Amir was romantic and kind. He wasn't interested in religion, and he was totally open to others. When our son was born, he jokingly asked, "Should we baptize him or whisper Allahu Akbar in his ear?" We named him Hawar, after the Kurdish soccer player. He once joked that a single soccer game was more important than any religious ritual. He never imposed anything on me, so I always said my Christian prayers.

When Mimi was born, I didn't know what to name her. She was just two weeks old when they put the letter N on the houses. I didn't have any particular names in mind. Instead of naming her, I decided to go in search of my husband, because it was said that some soldiers were being held captive by Daesh. I wondered if maybe he was just being held, that he wasn't dead, even though his friend had said that they threw their bodies into the river ...

Some injuries we can't really express, we can only feel ...

I asked Umm Ahmad if I could leave my son and daughter with her while I went to look for their father. She agreed, and advised me to wear a black veil to avoid harassment from Daesh, which I did. I took a taxi to his workplace in the Yarmouk Center in the Tanak District. It was the first time I'd ever been to his work. Two young men were standing at the door. "I've come to ask about my husband," I said. One of them, who looked like he was seventeen years old, asked what my husband's name was. "Amir," I replied. "We didn't kill or detain anyone," he said. I was about to leave when a black Toyota pulled up in front of the building. Somebody stepped out of the car and walked toward me, asking the two others, "Who's she?" The same person who'd spoken to me answered, "She came to ask about her husband. He used to work here." Then the man said, "So he's a traitor." I felt nervous when I heard him say this, and I adjusted the veil on my head. When I did so, he saw the tattoo on my hand, a cross my mom had given me when I was a child. He yanked on my hand, and said, "So, you're a Christian?" I didn't know how to answer, so he added, "All the Christians left the city. Why are you still here? You must be a trap for us." He dragged me inside and pulled the veil off my head. "How sweet. Where's your family?" he asked. "I don't know," I answered. He didn't believe me. Then he asked, "And who's your husband's family?" I said I didn't know. Then he asked me, "Do you have any children?" I didn't answer. They tied my hands behind my back and imprisoned me in a room all by myself. They left me there for two days without food or drink. After that, they came back and asked me, "So, are you going to confess now?" I asked, "Confess to what?" Then one of them approached me and said, "I know how to make her talk." He untied my hands, which had become swollen. He put a needle under my nail and peeled it off – to this day, when my nail grows, it bends up on its own. Then he brought a box cutter to hack off my fingers. Seconds before doing so, the other man said, "Let her be. She's beautiful. We can sell her, a beautiful sabya." He shoved me so hard that my head hit the window. I lost consciousness, and didn't feel anything until I found myself in a school filled with other captives. They were girls of all ages, from ten to sixty, and most of them were Yazidis. After three days there I saw a ten-year-old girl named Lalish. She was exceptionally beautiful. Her braid was still tied the way her mother had done it for her. They took her away at night, didn't bring her back until morning. She came back with dried blood all over her feet. She was trying to walk but kept falling to the ground. She was naked, and they threw her clothes on top of her. I put her clothes on for her. At night, she fell ill with a high fever. The way she looked, I thought she might not see morning. I hugged her and made cold compresses for her. I felt attached to her because she was about Hawar's age. Every minute she said, "Oh, Mom." She was moaning like that for a full two months ...

Every day I remember her. I can't forget about her ...

A week later, someone opened the door and troubled everyone – he said, "We want fresh girls." He took me and Azab, a girl who was younger than me, twenty-eight years old. He raped us both. His name is Farouk al-Shammari. Then he took us to another room. Two men entered. They spoke a language I didn't understand. They were partying – doing drugs and drinking – and they raped us, taking turns, one after another. Farouk raped me four times in one day. Azab was a virgin, and she got pregnant. She and I didn't talk to each other, we only cried together. They married and divorced us eight times on the same day, and they made us wear porno outfits. We were too tired to resist. We didn't say a word. Tears flowed down our cheeks. The last time I glanced at Azab, she looked at me and bit her finger ...

That bite comes to my mind every once in a while ...

The worst humiliation I ever felt was the morning that we were taken to the assembly hall outside the school. They didn't let us wear our clothes. We came outside naked, and the guards harassed us and hit us. They raped us there in that assembly hall however they wished. One day they sold me to an ugly man named Sufyan. I screamed at him, "I hate you." As revenge, he burned my chest with an ember, saying, "This is so you'll remember me for your whole life."

(Claudia showed me the burn on her chest: "Whenever I take a shower and see this, I do remember him.")

I wasn't the only one to attempt suicide. A lot of other captives did as well. A woman in her sixties prevented me from killing myself. I call her Mama Adhra. She always offered me hope and compassion. She even gave my daughter her name

– she's the one who named her Maryam. She would talk to me, and pray for me as if she were a saint of our time, even though she was sometimes being raped herself. Whenever she turned up crying I knew she had been raped. One time she left and didn't come back for two days. I was beside myself, especially after Farouk came and said that they'd sold all of us to someone from Saudi Arabia named Khaldoun, and that he would come to pick us up in three days. I was so relieved when she returned safely before the sale. I didn't want to be sold without Mama Adhra.

The day after Mama Adhra returned, somebody shouted at me, "Auntie Claudia?" I turned around, and to my surprise, I saw Ahmad, the son of the neighbor that I'd left my kids with. I didn't know he was with Daesh, but still I was happy to see him. My joy didn't last more than a minute, though. He pushed me aside and walked away. Maybe he had killed my kids, I thought, maybe he thinks of me as an infidel – why else would he have shoved me like that? Mama Adhra tried to calm me. "Maybe he pushed you so that they don't get suspicious about him, because he called you auntie in front of them," she said. Ahmad actually came back that same day, and tossed a small scrap of paper my way. Mama Adhra picked it up before I could and quickly hid it in her clothes. "Come on, let's go the bathroom," she said. There she unfolded the paper: "Auntie Claudia, wait for me tonight by the window."

I waited by the window but he didn't come before I fell asleep. Apparently Mama Adhra couldn't sleep. She woke me up at dawn when Ahmad arrived. "I want to help you, but I need money for the smugglers," he told me. "I have gold stored above the ceiling in the bathroom. The key is under the trash can out in front of the house," I replied.

I waited for Ahmad to come and tell me about the escape plan, or about anything at all. Five days passed and I lost hope once again because they'd decided to take us to Syria. They brought three buses – the girls were all weeping as they packed us inside, and when the bus started moving, I felt my hope drawing farther and farther away. They stopped the bus for an hour at the Syrian border because the merchants who'd bought us hadn't arrived yet. While we were stopped there, a tall man came onto the bus and asked, "Which one of you is Claudia?" I said, "Leave me alone, please, may God protect you." But he ordered me to follow him. We walked toward the valley, and I was terrified when I glimpsed four young men waiting for us. I thought they were going to rape me. As we approached, I saw that Ahmad was with them. I felt as if I were rising from the dead, or as if a second opinion of an X-ray showed that the first reading had been incorrect, and that the presumed disease didn't exist after all. I ran to him.

"Go down through this valley, they'll help you in that Syrian village down there," he said.

"But where are my kids?" I asked him, "I want to see them."

"Do you know how dangerous this is?" he replied.

"Why don't we put her in the trunk of the car?" the boy standing next to Ahmad suggested.

"I'm afraid we'll get caught," Ahmad said.

I just stood there while they remained silent. Then I started walking toward the valley. After I'd gone a short distance, they pulled up to me in their car and opened the trunk. I got in. The car weaved into traffic with other cars and buses. I felt like I was going to suffocate. Every now and then they lifted the back seat to make sure I was still breathing. One of them said, "I'm scared to death – what if they find her in the car?"

Then he got out of the car, and told Farouk, who was leading the group, "Our car is old, and I'm afraid we'll be late, so why don't we get out first?" Farouk gave him the okay, and they sped off. They said they'd drop me off in the Tammouz District in Mosul.

They did that quickly, and then went away. My house was in the Yarmouk District, fifteen minutes away by car. In Mosul, it was dangerous for a woman to be on the street without a head scarf, so I flagged down a taxi, but didn't have any money. I was in such bad shape that the driver asked, "What's the matter?"

"I don't know what to do. My son is missing. Maybe he's with his grandfather?" I replied.

"Why isn't your head covered? Daesh is going to be upset with us," he said.

"There's no time. I have to find my son," I replied.

A few minutes later, the Daesh police stopped him. I was about to die from fear. "She's sick, poor thing," he told them. They let us pass after advising me that I should cover my head.

When I arrived at my house, I told the driver, "I'll find you some money."

"The world isn't that rotten. Go on, I don't want anything," he replied.

I knocked on my neighbor's door. My son Hawar opened it. He was shocked to see me as I hugged him.

"I thought I didn't have a father or a mother anymore," he said.

Ahmad's mother greeted me with kisses. She told me that Hawar was taking good care of his sister, and that every time she cried he'd say, "She just wants her mother."

I told Umm Ahmad what had happened. She broke into tears, shocked to learn that Ahmad worked with Daesh. "He said he was very busy because he had found a new job," she said.

She wouldn't let me leave her house. I stayed with her for a month. She lived with her husband and their two daughters. They bought me a cell phone. Umm Ahmad called her son but he didn't answer. He later left her a voice message saying that he'd sold my gold for ten thousand dollars, and that he'd paid smugglers to get me out of Mosul because it was too dangerous for me to stay there, as a Christian. I dialed the number he left in his message, and the person who picked up told me when I should leave for Kurdistan, and also recommended that I take water and diapers with me. Hawar carried the water, and I carried Mimi. Just before leaving their home, I called Ahmad and asked him, "I have one last request for you. Please, tell me, where did they take those three buses? I want to know what happened to Lalish. She's never far from my mind."

"Those buses were sold to Saudi Arabia. Some of the girls were used for service, others would be sold for their organs and body parts." Umm Ahmad was staring at me, she could probably tell from the look on my face that Ahmad just told me something awful. But I didn't say anything and just hugged her goodbye.

We walked in a convoy of about a hundred people, most of them Muslims fleeing Mosul with their families to protect their daughters from Daesh. We walked toward Kirkuk without food for three days. The sound of gunshots was louder at night. Someone shouted, "Down on the ground, everyone!" We did just that.

It was too dark to see anything. When the sound of gunfire subsided, people started walking in all directions. In that moment, I looked left and right without seeing Hawar – he'd refused to be held by the hand because he thought he was a big boy. I couldn't believe that this could happen, that my son could disappear in a flash. I started screaming and crying, not knowing what to do when the caravan started moving again. My son was lost in the cold and darkness, so quietly and unbelievably. It was as if he knew something was going to happen. That day, he'd even kissed and hugged me – he didn't usually do that. He even said, "I love you."

I can't sleep. Whenever I flee to bed, Hawar appears in my dreams. When I wake up and don't find him here, I go crazy …

I waited there until I wound up at the back of the convoy. But I still couldn't find Hawar. People were curling like waves and I was soaked in my own disaster. Their stream carried me along as I held Maryam and looked everywhere in hopes of finding Hawar. Later, in the camp, they took me to see Umm Raad, who reads fortunes out of the dictionary. She told me he was with an old woman who was taking care of him, and that he was looking for me. I could only hope that her intuition was correct.

At the Erbil checkpoint, the policeman objected to my passing through. "Why don't you have an identity card?" he asked me. "You can't pass without one."

I collapsed in tears, saying, "I'm the one who gets to ask you: Why don't I have an identity? Daesh rapes us, takes away our IDs, and you hold me accountable, not them?"

I'm scared, I always feel that Daesh is lurking behind the door. I miss my father so desperately. One day he told me, "Never put your head down. Look at that bright star, and remember that I'm close to you, no matter how far away I go." Answer me, Dad, with a hug just like every time, or even hit me, if you please. Just answer me.

It was midnight, and the owner of the café wanted to close. In Claudia's tearful eyes, I saw the world evaporating, and didn't know what to do. She had to get back to the camp, so we left together, with Maryam in the middle holding our hands and still humming the song "Daddy Finger."

I woke up at dawn and couldn't fall back asleep. I'd had a strange dream. A man was playing the piano. Suddenly he stood up in anger, bumped into the table as he turned around, scattering all the books that were on top of it. I was upset because I had arranged them there.

In the morning Abdullah asked me how much longer I was going to stay in Iraq.

"Only a couple more hours," I told him.

"No, that can't be right. What a short visit."

"I know. How is it going today?"

"Do you want to come to the market with me?"

"Sure. I want to buy some gifts."

"Do you want to pass by the Office of Kidnapped Affairs first, or just go straight to the market?"

"This would be a good opportunity to stop by the office."

"The director, Hussein Koro, is a very nice person and a friend of mine. You can ask him anything you want, he'll be happy to meet with you."

There, Mr. Hussein shook my hand, smiling. There was a flag of Kurdistan behind him. "I heard from Abdullah that you visited Lalish and some of the camps," he said.

"That's right. The people in the camps overwhelmed me with their spirit of hospitality," I said.

"Someone from a foreign humanitarian organization said, *These people are weird: we came to help them, and yet they offer*

us water and food, insisting that we have some tea with them.
Even during the Daesh invasion, some Muslims sought shelter
in Sinjar, fleeing with the people of the region up to the mountains. After fifteen days of siege up on the mountain, a helicopter came and took the families to the Feshkhabur zone near the
Iraqi-Syrian border. People in the area told the Muslims: *You
are guests, please, you go first into the helicopter.* Customs of
hospitality are deeply rooted in our area, you know."

"I guess this office didn't exist before Daesh."

"It was established to facilitate the work of local rescuers
(such as Abdullah), who were working out of their personal ini-
tiative and coordinating between families and external smugglers who were in Daesh areas. We opened a dossier of missing
persons and their details. By the numbers: 6,386 persons are
kidnapped or missing; 3,527 of them are females; 2,587 have
returned so far, including 934 women and 325 men, 658 female
children and 670 male children. That means 3,799 people are
still in the hands of Daesh. These are the latest statistics dated
May 15, 2016. Daesh calls our men prisoners of war and our
women sabaya. After they rape the sabya, they call her *jariya*,
or female servant. At that point it becomes their right to buy
or sell her in the slave market, and the price ranges from one
dollar to five hundred dollars. After that, if the seller wants her
back, he can make a deal with the buyer to return her to him.
But first he must sell her, at least once, before he can possess
her. That's their law. Those slave markets currently exist in the
cities of Mosul, Talafar, and Raqqa. Some of these markets
exist on the Internet, opening and closing at specific times, like
any market. Some of them are purchased for personal whims,
some for service, and some (by people like Abdullah) for the
purpose of bringing them back to their families."

"You listen to the stories of survivors for the sake of documentation," I said. "Does this work affect you psychologically?"

"Of course, it does affect me. Sometimes I can't sleep. Imagine, for example, what it would be like to listen to a nine-year-old girl explain how she was raped even though she didn't know what sex was. She says, *I don't know why they were doing that to me. No one had ever laid a hand on me before.*"

After leaving the office and the market, Abdullah suggested that we sit in a café until it was time for me to go. We ordered ice cream, but it melted before we could eat it. I didn't know why we'd gotten it in the first place.

"Abdullah, I need to ask you something: Will the publication of this book cause any harm to you or to anyone mentioned in it?" I said.

"No," he firmly replied.

"Scheherazade saved her life with the tales she told. You, on the contrary, may be putting your own life at risk because of these tales."

"You mean I'm like Scheherazade? I'd be happy to be like Scheherazade. Listen, I have a gift for you."

"I wonder what it could be."

"Natural honey."

"Where did you get it? I thought you weren't beekeeping anymore."

"I brought it from Sinjar. I have a friend there who keeps bees. I go there to help him sometimes. I'm nostalgic for bees. How I love to watch their patterns of flight, circle by circle, as the queen flies higher and higher ..."

I remembered the wonderful song of Fairouz, "The Path of Bees" (the path of flying bees / over the broken light / drawing circles / writing lines in the air / high above the palaces / higher than the domes, drawing lines / if you're going to leave me darling / remember me / and remember the path of bees). I daydreamed a bit with the circles of bees, all the way back to circles of childhood that we used to draw in the dirt with a little stick, circular ripples of waves that grow bigger when we toss a stone into the water, rings of fire that tigers jump through at the circus, the circles of whirling Sufi dervishes who spin and spin until they disappear, the circles my brother drew on a piece of paper when he lost his memory after a stroke, circles made in the air by a little girl as she skipped rope in the camp.

"This is the nicest gift. Thank you. I hope next time I visit you'll be back home in Sinjar with your farm and your bees," I said.

"Of course we want the region to be fully liberated so that we can return to our past lives. But, in fact, something inside us has changed forever. Some people will never return. On the other hand, this disaster has opened our eyes to some beautiful stances and wonderful people …

Abdullah began again: As your Scheherazade, before I accompany you to the airport, let me tell you another story of a girl who is a relative of mine. I visited her family a week ago to offer my condolences for her death, or rather, her suicide. Can you believe that after she survived Daesh and arrived safely here, she killed herself just like that?

Jamila was living in one of the caves in Sinjar with her mother, her father, and her younger sister. They were somewhat isolated – they didn't have a clock; they would wake up to the sound of the rooster, and go to sleep when the stars appeared in the sky. Sons and daughters in the village usually helped their parents with everything, including farming, milking the cows, and taking care of the chickens. Every day Jamila would ride their donkey to fetch water for the family. Once, her donkey stopped in front of another donkey coming from the opposite direction. A young man was sitting on top of the other one. The two donkeys seemed to know each other, which made Jamila and the boy smile, but then they each went on their way. Jamila kept smiling to herself, thinking of that tan young man who'd turned his face to glance at her after she'd left. The days passed, and Jamila would go off and come back with her donkey, as usual, until one day she caught a glimpse of a donkey coming toward her from the opposite direction with a rider she knew – it was as if she'd known him for a long time. They slowed down as they got closer to each other, then both stopped. He smiled and said hello. She greeted him in return. He asked her where she was bringing her water from. When she told him, he said that he knew of a spring where the water was purer, and offered to show it to her. She followed him. There, they dismounted from the donkeys, and drank the spring water from their cupped hands. "This water really is better, I'll take some home to my family," she said. "Who is your family?" he asked. They told each other about themselves and their lives, as if they were old friends. When Jamila got home with the new water, she felt like something had touched her soul, something she had never felt before – it was as if the handful of water she'd drunk had magically transformed her into a happy human being who loved everything around her; she found such a mysterious beauty in it all. The next day, when she went to this new spring, she found the man sitting there. He didn't say that he'd been waiting for her, but that he'd been there since morning. They sat talking on a rock beside the water. He touched her hand, and she felt her heart pounding. "Did you want to tell me something?" he asked.

"What about you? Did you want to say something to me?" she said.

"I have a secret. Let's keep it between you and me."

"What is it?"

"I think my donkey is in love with yours."

"Really? How did you know?"

"He lost his mind. It's as if he's gone crazy."

"How so?"

"He stays up all night, waiting for the sun to come up, so that he can come to this spring."

"Same with my donkey. Nothing pleases him except coming back to this spring."

"I stay up with him every night. I can't sleep."

"Why not?"

"I look up at the stars, thinking of a girl I'm in love with. I ask the stars, *Does she love me too?*"

"What do the stars tell you?"

"They tell me to just ask her, to ask the girl I'm in love with. So, let me ask you, *Jamila, what do the stars say?*"

"Each star says, *I love you.*"

After continuing to meet at the spring, they decided to get married. On this special day he took her to a house made of mud, next to his family's house. He said it would be their home in the near future. He'd intended to bring his family with him so he could ask for her hand after the month of April had ended. Their custom prohibited marriages that month because, as the saying goes, only nature can be a bride in April, and you can't have two brides at once; and the earth mustn't be plowed in April because it is pregnant with colorful flowers and wild plants during that time of year.

Jamila eagerly awaited the end of the month. She desperately wanted for the two of them to "become one," as he put it.

He joked with her about the wedding, saying, "I wonder how musicians and drummers will be able to get through the rugged, mountainous areas to reach your house, and the two donkeys will have to lead the wedding procession."

Jamila told her mother that they would have guests over to discuss the engagement. Her mother inquired about the man's last name and origin, which was the tradition for mothers in those situations. Once the month was over, however, a quarrel broke out between the young man's parents, which led to his mother leaving to go to her family's house. The family's drama wasn't conducive to the engagement, so it was postponed.

One day, when Jamila was on her way to the spring to meet him, Daesh kidnapped her. They took her to Talafar, where she was sold along with the other captives. Jamila curled up as tightly as she could to resist being raped, but the man who claimed to own her took her by force, and made her bleed. Jamila wept bitterly, wondering how her lover would react if he ever found out that she was no longer a virgin. *He loves me, so he will have to forgive me*, she thought to herself, *it isn't my fault*.

More than a year and a half after her kidnapping, he still hadn't left her mind for a moment. Sometimes she imagined him coming on his donkey to save her, and she would hold onto him as the donkey raced away like a motorcycle. Her mind carried her to that little mud house, where she would wash his clothes and cook for him, and she would give birth to children who looked like him. Her hope of returning to him allowed her to withstand the torture of captivity. She didn't try to commit suicide, as some of the captives who were in the building with her did. She resisted death for his sake.

Daesh locked up more than just people – they captured animals as well. They imprisoned goats, cows, and chickens from the village, forcing them into captivity as well. Once, a Daeshi came and asked the captives, "Do any of you know how to milk a cow?" Jamila and three other women replied that they did, and so they were moved in with the cows. They thought this might exempt them from being raped, but they discovered that milking cows was just extra work, and didn't keep them from being sold, bought, or raped. After three and a half months of living in that place near the barn, they'd milked the cows as many times as they'd been raped – the time came for the four of them to escape. They had an hour to do it, so one of them suggested a plan, and the rest quickly agreed to it. They put on Daesh clothes and the men's head covering, the *yashmagh*. It was winter so they put on coats as well. The clothes smelled foul, but it was all they could find.

The four girls headed west toward Sinjar, which was fifteen miles away. They reminded each other to behave like men, in case someone saw them or stopped them along the way. They walked for an hour until they arrived at an abandoned farm, where they decided to rest. They were shrouded in complete darkness, but they noticed lights coming from the direction they had fled. The lights seemed to be heading toward them, so they jumped up and ran away. They found a trench nearby, where they decided to hide, scattering dirt and grass on top of themselves. The lights came closer and were fixed on the farm that they'd just left. A spotlight came so close that it brought their breathing to a halt. Then the spot-light continued past them to the other side, before it gradu-ally disappeared. They came out of the trench, brushed the dried grass out of one another's hair, and walked toward the mountains until morning. There, by the valley at the foot of the mountain, they sat to rest, exhausted from hunger, thirst, and fear. They fell asleep until noon, and when they woke up, they saw a car coming toward them in the distance. One of them suggested that they flag down the car to see if they could get some water, at least, but the others objected out of fear. Every now and then, one of them would walk a little ways from the valley and then come back. Gradually, the sun went down, and they headed west. Their thirst became unbearable. Every time one of them collapsed to the ground from thirst, she would tell the others to move on and leave her there, but they all kept their promise to stay together. Suddenly they arrived at a house that looked abandoned. Hesitantly creeping inside, they found it was empty, except for the one thing they so desperately wanted: a water basin. They drank from it, and then washed their faces. They felt life returning to them. They sat on the floor to rest for a moment, but ended up falling asleep – and they didn't wake up until they heard the sound of dawn prayer. They left the house and walked all the way to the village of Sinno, but when they saw cars flying Daesh black flags there, they froze, and didn't move from where they were in the valley. They stayed there until darkness fell, until all the cars disappeared. They found bodies and human remains dumped beside the road. One of them fell down and refused to keep walking. The rest of them slowed down and stayed with her until she calmed down a bit. In that moment, Jamila found a soft spot of grass in the valley, and she concluded that there must be water there. She dug into the ground until she found it. "This is spring water, come drink it," she said. The water was mixed with mud, but they were so thirsty and their lips were so dry. Each took a handful of water and wetted her lips. They kept walking toward the mountains. Despite the darkness, they could see fighters up there. Happily, they ran toward them, but those fighters fired shots toward the girls, thinking they were with Daesh. The girls forgot that they were disguised as Daesh. They were in quite a predicament: every time they moved they would hear the whiz of bullets flying by. Finally, one of them decided to take off her clothes – she threw away the *yashmagh*, let down her long hair, and only left on her pants. She ascended the mountain waving her hands in the air. Some of the fighters ran toward her. She pointed out the other girls to them. Each fighter carried a girl on his back and climbed back up the mountain. They carried them on their backs for two miles, to the headquarters of the Sinjar protection forces. They remained up in the mountains for a few days under the care of Sinjaris.

Jamila wanted to surprise her lover. She wore a dress with colorful flowers on it, and got ready to see him. She smiled thinking about the mud house adjacent to his parents' house. In her mind, she wondered how he was going to receive her. Would he pick her up with joy, like someone in a movie? Would he cry upon hearing about the torture she endured in captivity? Did he even know that she had been kidnapped? Or did he think that she was dead?

Her mother welcomed her with tears, hugging her for a long time, in disbelief that her daughter returned. Jamila was waiting to hear something about her beloved, who'd asked for her hand in marriage two years earlier. She dared to ask her mother whether she had heard anything about him. "He's okay ..." she said, and then fell silent. Jamila looked expectantly at her mother, waiting for her to say more. Her mother added, "He got married a month ago."

Jamila didn't say anything, she didn't betray any emotion. After an hour of doing nothing, she went out to walk around the streets of her village. But what had happened to those streets? Why were they wrapped around her like an octopus? Nothing was the same anymore, even the sky had changed, it wasn't the way it was supposed to be. The world had changed around her, at the exact moment when she most desired her old, familiar things.

Her steps accelerated as her thoughts floated upward. She ran down the dirt road, gasping for air. Her breath was cut short, as if the hands of her rapists had all come back together and were choking her to death, beating her, insulting her, shoving her into the corner.

Their hands tore her body into two halves, like two countries at war, the dividing line an inferno and dead people ...

Her dress exploded,
the flowers scattered in the air,
the colors popped up high like fireworks in a celebration,
but; no sound could be heard,
no sound ...